The Woman at the Well

Pastor Evelyn Sanders

The Woman at the Well
Pastor Evelyn Sanders

Published by:
KPG Book Publishing
(a division of Kingdom Publishing Group, Inc.)
P.O. Box 505, Ashland, VA 23005
www.kingdompublishing.org
info@kingdompublishing.org

Library of Congress
Copyright © 2006; 2009

by: Pastor Evelyn Sanders
Come And See Ministries Inc.

ISBN 13: 978-0-9824084-1-4
ISBN 10: 0-9824084-1-2

"Am I Not The Same" poem by Jonathan Mackey

Cover Design: by Herbert L. Brown
Co-editor: Gloria Pace-Allen
Scriptures: King James Edition-The Holy Bible

All Rights Reserved.
No part of this book may be reproduced. his book or parts thereof may not be reproduced in any form, without written permission of the author and/or publisher, except as provided by the United States of America copyright law.

Printed in the United States of America.

In Memoriam

In memory of my Mom, Juanita Foreman, who left me with words of wisdom.

"If you can't add to a person don't take from them." These are words that can carry a generation. I thank God for her unwavering faith in me that caused me to accomplish the mission that He has set before me. I give thanks to my mom who believed in her daughter. I miss her lovely spirit and voice that never changed from the time I was a little one.

In memory of my daughter, Thomasina Camille Owens, who left the Word of God in the hearts of many souls saying, *"We know that all things work together for good to them that love God, to them who are the called according to his purpose"* (Romans 8:28).

Dedications

This book is dedicated to:

God, my husband and my children. My husband Richard has been my mentor since we have been married. He has pushed me to passion and purpose. He believed in whatever I was doing and encouraged me to further my life in education and ministry. His words of wisdom have kept me in line with the word of God. For every pit stop there was a word from the Lord. His patience and love is my reward for writing without interruption. He never complained but waited on me in my endeavor to complete the work. I thank you Richard for your enduring love that you poured into me for this purpose in life.

My daughter, Thomasina, a wonderful woman of God who believed in her mother and asked God to let me write when I got writer's block. She encouraged me to look for publishers and sent away for information for me. She would listen to my stories and thought that they were good. In the midst of my writing she had a Holy Trinity Shut In at her home. She asked me to read some of the stories from "The Woman at the Well". I was so grateful that before the book was published it was being used for God's glory. Many of the women that were there got healed. Thank you Thomasina for believing in your mom.

My son Jonathan a great writer that has not been discovered has encouraged me by writing with me. We both like to share our writing one of his favorite writings is,"<u>I Am the Same</u>."

My children Am I not the same God who delivered you, I am the same who sought to save you from yourself, the same who washed you, clothed you, and set you on solid ground. Why then would I leave you in the midst of your journey when it was I who started you on your way, I am the same and I will not deny you the truth. Trust, Trust, trust, trust me and I will walk before you and give you confident for I am the keeper of all things. Cling to your spirit, which is like me, there lies your hope there lie your riches. Do not fear me just because I hold the key and the deed to your house, but fear me out of reverence. Children am I not the same God I was when you cried out to me, never will I leave you never will I break a promise. Charge me if you will my words are sweet, even to my ears remember our friendship and speak to me as Father and Friend for I am the same.

Jonathan, thank you for your words of wisdom that encouraged me to write.

My son Gabriel I thank you for being behind the scene praying and remembering all that I have said and respected me as your mother.

Most of all, my Father in Heaven who I honor. You put the revelation of his love in me to write about the "Woman At The Well" and gave the insight of women and their purpose. I thank you Father for your love and mercy that kept me focused and all the souls you put in my path to stir up the gift that you had placed in me. I am forever grateful to my God and my Father for all that He has done and what He is about to do. Thank You Father, for your love.

Acknowledgements

These are the women who were there to help me stand in the liberty where I was set free. They are wells of living water that poured into me while I was writing this book. Each one of them is special and unique in their own way. They are behind the scene but their wisdom speaks loud. As you read these stories I pray that you will be in contact with a well. The well will bring safety if you embrace it. Get ready for your water release.

Their wisdom and understanding showed me how to stay focused while writing this book. This has been a wonderful experience for me and I am challenged to continue writing books

Stella Hunter is a friend that sticks closer than a brother. She is behind the scene. I don't see her often, but we are close as sharing daily bread. Her friendship has been one that held me close to God, because of her integrity and consistency in relation to the Father of heaven. She loves at all times and truth is on her lips. She is a wonderful friend in deeds and truth. She was there when all had forsaken me. She believed in my quest to serve the Lord at all cost. I thank God for a friend and I thank you Stella for sharing your time and life when I needed it the most.

Another one of my close friends is a woman of vision. Christina Walls a woman that has progress, passion, and purpose in front of her. She is a builder and she tears down anything that's not like God. She rises as the virtuous woman and goes and does her daily task. I met Christina when I working many years ago and didn't know the impact she would have on my life. God uses her to birth promises for his glory. She spoke into my life and saw the potential and said, "You can do it". She prophesied over me to go to college and I finish with honors. She poured into me over and over and pushed me into my destiny. I am grateful to the mighty woman of God who has labored with me to complete these stories. Thanks Christina for your obedience to God remembering that we are our brother's keeper.

Hazel Hall is a wonderful woman of God. Thank you for being there and believing in me when the chips were down, Hazel is a woman that pulls out the wisdom that you have and teaches you while she is doing it. She is a well that many women can draw from. Thank you Hazel for your love and all that you have done and said to encourage me.

Tina Payne-Brissette a great woman of God and a great writer helped me with some of the editing of this book. I was blessed to be able to have an established editor to look at my work and admired it. Thanks again for your love and kindness you showed toward me. I appreciate everything you have done.

My sister and a mighty woman of God Therese DeMartin encouraged me to write in the midst of her pain and trials she had words of wisdom to help me. She is a young woman that has been without the use of her legs for some time but her spirit is full of life. Her miracle is at the door and I am grateful to God for this great woman of God that has the strength to know that Whatever God has said He will perform it. Thanks Terry for your love and kindness you poured on me.

There are many souls that help me to complete this work that are not mention, but God knows each soul that sowed a nugget and He will not forget. I give thanks to all the women that will read this material and gleam from it.

Preface

These lessons in life are purposed to build on the foundation that has already been laid by Jesus Christ. We have been instructed by God to bring forth fruit that will remain.

God said, "Go ye therefore, and teach all nations, baptizing them in the name of the Father and of the Son, and of the Holy Ghost: Teaching them to observe all things whatsoever I have commanded you: and, lo I am with you always, even unto the end of the world. Amen." (Matthew 28:19-20).

Woman at the Well is designed to bring souls to the Kingdom of God. It contains model characters, each portrayed in different circumstances and lifestyles, in scenes depicting life's struggles that draw each of them to the well in need of the living water.

God came to heal the broken hearted, to proclaim liberty to the captive, and to open the prison to those who are bound. She is a church that was designed to bring souls to the Kingdom of God. Her messenger is from the beginning to the end.

Contents

Preface 9
Introduction 13

Part One: Personal Experiences

Marie's Story *19*
Judy's Story *23*
Jennifer's Story *25*
Joan's Story *27*
Clean Woman *29*
Gossip Woman *33*
Jealous Woman *35*
Stone Woman *37*
Women of Zion *39*
Destiny *43*

Part Two: Awesome Women

Sarah *47*
Esther *49*
Ruth *51*
Rahab *53*
Lot's Wife *55*
Hannah *57*
Mary *59*

Part Three: Season of Life

Josephine *63*
Luke Warm *65*
Woman of Issues *67*
Bread Winners *69*
Alabaster Box *73*
Water Your Marriage *77*
Spiritual Bankrupt *79*

Cluttered Soul	81
Silent Frustration	83
Love Bug	85
Vashti (Conceited woman)	87
The Woman Left Desolate	89
The Grieving Woman	91
The Weary Soul	93
Odious Woman	95
The Twin Identity	97
Heartache Woman	99

Part Four: Overcoming Women

Over coming Woman	103
Women of Submission	105
Deborah	107
Grandmothers Challenges	109
Anna	111
Naomi	113
Program Woman	115
The Bleeding woman of Grief	117
Insecure Woman	119
The Stage woman	121
Red Hat Women	125
The Virtuous Woman	127

About the Author 127

Introduction

The woman at the well is one, which consists of many facets. Her character portrays that of a woman in need of a father. A father is one, who nurtures, protects, and provides security. Her message goes out to the North, the South, the East, and the West to ends of the earth. As we approach her story we will see her quest for a father.

We see her as a woman that has lost her foundation and her identity, as she walks to the well with her head held in a slumped position, heavily laden waiting for a breakthrough in her life at this time. Her face is weary and tearful and drawn with tension. Her thoughts left her preoccupied with all the prior relationships that she had experienced.

She did not have a father in her background. She had silent frustrations; her soul was cluttered with all her past experiences with men. Men represent her idea of what a father could be. But, left her dry, and heart broken. Her relationships became apparent and more vivid to the community; because she would go to the well alone when the sun was at its highest; so that she would not encounter the gossiping woman, who had labeled her as a woman of the night, a woman who they defined as a promiscuous woman.

She was seeking life in all her relationships with her husbands. Her heart was looking for the coming Messiah the one that would tell her all things. As she approached the well, and looked up, she did not recognize Jesus at the well until he spoke, and asked her for a drink of water. And she replied, "you know the Jews have no dealings with the Samaritans.""Jesus, answered and said if thou knew the gift of God and say unto thee, Give me a drink, thou would have asked of him to give me a drink of living water. Sir, I have nothing to draw with, and the well is deep: from whence then has thou hast thou, that living water? And Jesus answered and said whosoever drink of the water that I shall give him should never thirst; but the water that I should give him, should be in him a well of water springing up into everlasting life" (John 4:10-14). The woman then replied for Jesus to give her the water. Jesus asked, go call your husband to come here, and she said, "I, have no husband." And Jesus let her know that the words she spoke were true. Because, she has had five husbands and the one she has now is not her husband. She then perceived that Jesus was a prophet.

Jesus had spoke into her life truth, which none had never spoken. In her quest for a father she had many marriages seeking for comfort and security as result of an absent father. By not having a father figure it caused her to seek comfort from her marriages. Marriage can be anything that you attach or bound yourself too. For example, a job, organization, recycling the decorative interior of your home, and family. When she met Jesus she examined the inside of her cavity (heart). "The woman saith unto him, I know that Messiah cometh, which is called Christ: when he is come, he will tell us all things. Jesus said unto her, 'I that speak unto thee Am He'" (John 4:25-26).

After being introduced to the Messiah she left her water pots to go tell her story and each character in this book portrays her journey in life until she finds the living water.

The woman at the well is a powerful message that will continue through out the ages. There will always be a need of a Savior. As you know God knows us from the beginning to the end.

A woman will continue to search for a well to drink from but until she finds the living eternal water they will always be thirsty. Each woman is a well full of information locked up inside of her. Jesus spoke to her spirit, person, and her gender. Her stories are never ending because each generation has a part of her to disclose of.

God inspired me to write "The Woman at the Well" by the many souls that I have come to minister at this point. This is a journey that God has put into my spirit, unlike the other books I have written this one is dear to me because I too was a woman that was in need of the living water. Are you in need of the living water?

This book will enlighten your heart because it was ordained by God to bring forth much fruit for the kingdom of God. This is a word of wisdom in due season that will alter the hearts of men and women alike for times and times to come.

> *"These things I command you,
> that ye love one another."*
> *(John 15:17)*

Personal
Experiences

> *"As long as I am in the world,
> I am the light of the world."*
> *(John 9:5)*

Personal Experiences

Marie's Story

Marie is a woman that had been under the teachings of God since the tender age of seven. As a result, she experienced blessings from God. She had many trials and tribulations at the tender age of sixteen. She became pregnant during her junior year of high school. When you are young you fear humiliation that you encounter from both your peers and society.

As you know, when you are "going through" a personal situation of this magnitude, the enemy will bring to you distorted and confusing views or circumstances to your mind.

Marie had her own plans for life like most young women. Young women have plans and dreams of their adulthood. Our role-playing with dolls to become wives and mothers becomes a vivid imagination and the desire becomes a reality. The false reality then stems from media; television, commercials, magazines, newspapers, actors and actresses, Hollywood movies, and celebrity heroes.

There is no visual substance for focus on a husband or father (i.e. Barbie Dolls). Marie had experience in caring for her sister's children prior to her initial pregnancy, which equipped her with knowledge on how to care for infants/toddlers.

Marie was encouraged by her parents to abort her pregnancy; she did not comply with their request. As a result of her personal decision she felt the only respectable thing to do in her situation was to obtain her own place of residence for her and her expecting child. She was still herself, a child at heart with limited knowledge of child bearing. Marie prayed often to God about the unknown mysteries that were occurring in her physical body.

The baby came early at seven months and had to be put into an incubator for six weeks. The baby weighed two pounds. During this time, she could not bond with the baby until it weighed at least five pounds. Upon bringing the baby home she encountered other complications. After the six week check up the doctor gave the baby an injection of penicillin. As a result, the baby lost his body temperature. The baby's body became cold to the touch. Marie rushed the baby to the hospital and then she recognized that this was going to be a journey in the life of motherhood. The baby's heart stopped and Marie had to massage it because he was so small and that brought bonding for the mother and child.

This is not the only trial Marie had because later in life she had two more children and still had no husband. She was like the Woman at the Well that needed to drink from the living water. God raised Marie up and gave her dignity back and she raised three children with God's help and they are now adults each one of them is Christian and God fearing.

God saved Marie to be a light unto all those who lost hope in their despair. God came for those that are lost. No matter what we encounter in life, God is able to deliver us to drink from the well of life.

Marie is now a teacher of the Word and is writing books to help others who were ensnared before they got started. Sometimes it's our purpose to go through trials so that God can show his power in our life. God knew that Eve would eat from the tree of knowledge of good and evil and He knew that He was the Creator. *Who knows the mind of God? And who has been his counselor?* These are some of the experiences that each generation will encounter as they endeavor to follow their purpose. God said let every man or women be fully persuaded in his or her mind. (Romans 14:5).

Living Water: For God so loved the world, that he gave his only begotten Son so whoever believeth in him should not perish, but have everlasting life (John 3:16). The Bible tells us as a man think in his heart, so is he. (Proverbs 23:7).

The word of God is tried and He is a shield to all those who trust in Him. When we are not rooted and grounded in the Word any message that comes along sounds good. The Bible tells us that anything that is not of faith is sin. Truth mixed with a lie cannot stand (Ephesians 3:17; Hebrews 4:2).

> *"As long as I am in the world,
> I am the light of the world."*
> *(John 9:5)*

Judy's Story

Judy is a young woman that has fallen prey to the enemy and was left homeless at an early age.

When you are left on the porch of a relative without clothes you are predestined for a need. She was twelve years old. As you know, at this age you are developing into a young woman and your teen years are approaching. When you are homeless you are looking for love in all the wrong places and you are trying to get your next meal and a warm place to lay your head. Judy met with rape and drugs on her journey, and later became a prostitute. When you are in despair you become hopeless. Judy became successful in her line of business but her heart said why me?

There is a question in all of us who come to the road in life where nothing matters. When your heart is broken that's when God will receive you. He said I will receive a broken heart and a contrite spirit. He said He would give unto us beauty for ashes, and oil of joy for mourning, the garment of praise for the spirit of heaviness; that they might be called trees of righteousness, the planting of the Lord, that he might be glorified (Isaiah 61:3). God has vessels of honour and dishonour. Hath not the potter power over the clay (Romans 9:21).

Judy met a woman of God that began to enlighten her about Jesus and how He died for our sins. The woman showed her scriptures from the Bible and how Jesus forgave the woman that was caught in the act of adultery. She read that He said, He that is without sin among you; let him first cast a stone at her. After everyone left He said unto her, Woman, where are those thine accusers? Hath no man condemned thee? She said, no man, Lord. And Jesus said unto her, neither do I condemn thee go, and sin no more. (John 8:7, 9, 11).

After reading these scriptures Judy was now ready to give her life to Christ. She recognized that Jesus came that we might have life and that He died so that all men and women could live through him. Judy came in contact with a well and as she began to drink from the fountain of living water God healed her and now she is a witness to go forth to bring much fruit for the kingdom of God. The Woman of God was in the right place at the right time to deliver a soul from the error of his way. Brethren, if any of you do err from the truth, and one converts him; let him know, that he, which converteth the sinner from the error of his way, shall save a soul from death, and shall hide a multitude of sins (James 5:19-20).

Living Water: Be ye angry, and sin not: let not the sun go down upon your wrath: neither give place to the devil (Ephesians 4:26-27).

Jennifer's Story

Jennifer full of life and a hero for her peers has come to the road of life with a crippling disease.

She is 35 years old and is a believer of our Lord and Saviour Jesus Christ. Her faith stands trial. Only God can take you through the fire and bring you out with victory.

She is a teacher of the Word in a Christian Academy. When you are popular, life can bring some things you cannot understand but God who is rich in mercy can do anything. All things are possible to him that believe. The Bible tells us that the Word of God is tried and he is a buckler to all those who trust in him (Psalms 19:30). When the trial of life comes, sometimes we are not prepared spiritually.

God has given us all power over all principalities and might, and dominion and every name that is named (Ephesians 1:20). He has made us alive through Christ so that we can receive. Sometimes we are operating in the gifts and these are given freely without repentance. The gift will work for others and sometimes will not work for you, and it is demonstrated when difficult times occur. God wants us to be a partaker in the fruit He has given to us.

Jennifer got bitter with God because the circumstances did not change quickly. When you think you know, sometimes you fall. God always reveals the dark side of us at a time we think not. As we grow in Christ, God begins to open up things that we could not handle early in life. The crippling disease came from her soul. We walk around and our soul is being pierced with darts and causes us to not function in our body. God said, above all things that thou mayest prosper and be in health, even as thy soul prosper. (3rd John: 2).

When we stop receiving affirmations it cripples us because some of us need to be affirmed by others. When we begin to manifest the fruit of the spirit we are not concerned about being affirmed.

Jennifer went to a meeting one night and when she got there she was the only one there. She confesses her faults and begins to talk about God in her pain. Her words were "I am a child of God, I have my rights and He promised me He would answer my prayers." She said, "He should stop playing games with me." As she continues to expound she mocks God as being a liar and not the truth. The pastor of the church told her "God is not a man that he should lie" (Numbers 23:19). He turned to the scripture in Malachi and the scripture reads; "Then they that feared the Lord spake often one to another: and the Lord hearkened, and heard it, and a book of remembrance was written before him that feared the Lord, and that thought upon his name" (Malachi 3:16). He spoke into her spirit and the anointed words of God began to free her soul from the hand of the enemy. She was very prideful and thought that nothing could befall her.

    The word of God is our spiritual food - without it we cannot function properly in our body, because God desires truth in the inner parts. He took her to the book of Acts and there we saw Cornelius' prayers being answered. He said unto him, "thy prayers and thine alms are come up for a memorial before God "(Acts 10:4).

    Sometimes the gift has taken more of our time than our time spent with God. Our first call is to prayer. God said, "Our house shall be called a house of prayer (Luke 19:46)." The pastor showed her many truths that would free her spirit. Jennifer repented and renewed her vows before God and now she is no longer cripple in her soul. We have to earnestly contend for the faith, which was once delivered unto the saints (Jude 3).

    Living Water: But seek ye first the kingdom of God, and his righteousness; and all these things shall be added unto you (Matthew 6:33).

Joan's Story (Frantic Woman)

Joan is a woman frustrated with life and believes God is not hearing her prayers. This is a very common scene. We all have our days of doubt and unbelief.

God has given us a way out because He said if we confess our sins; He is faithful and just to forgive us our sins and to cleanse us from all unrighteousness (1 John 1:9).

Joan is a single parent and has two children, one son and one daughter. Her son has become rebellious against her teaching. When there is one parent in the home the children will hate the parent left raising them or they will blame the mother for the father not being there. Joan has been shaken; she lost her job, developed fluid on her brain causing her equilibrium to be off, her son is now a working adult but does not share in the needs of the home. He has also abused telephone privileges in her home by charging one thousand dollars that she was responsible for paying. She is a woman that needs to drink from the fountain of living waters. She went to the authorities to file the proper paper work to remove him from her home. Her heart is torn because he is her suckling child. God said, "Father, forgive them for they know not what they do" (Luke 23:34).

Our words create the environment we live in. Whatsoever we ask in prayer and believe, God hears (Mark 11:24). But when our heart has become a stone with iniquity God will not answer our prayer. The heart of God is mercy. Joan is a born again believer and loves the Lord, but her heart wants her son out of her sight. When you are afflicted in the body it turns your spirit into another person if you are not rooted and grounded in the Word. The Bible tells us that only peace can keep our hearts and minds through Christ Jesus (Philippians 4:7). When you are out of peace you are out of control. We need to keep our fruit in check at all times. God said guard your heart for out of it is the issues of life (Proverbs 4:23).

During the midst of her storm she had been praying for nine years that God would give her a vacation to Costa Rica. Immediately after she lost her job God released her to go to Costa Rica. Joan is now questioning God asking, "How can I go without money?" Her pastor gave her a word of knowledge that God has given her favor and she received it and said thank you. Not many days later she received her income tax check and even though she had need of other things God had favored her to go. She had met an old friend years ago from the Internet so she looked him up and there was room in the inn for her. After she arrived the room had been cancelled because of a family emergency. Her friend found her another room with a woman that believed in God. They prayed together, went sightseeing and visited the craters. While she was there she became overwhelmed with God's presence and how great He is. Sometimes we need to go away in order to see the goodness of God. She saw His hand in every place she stepped. When you turn your face away from your circumstances you can see God.

Living Water: Oh! That men would praise the Lord for his goodness, and for his wonderful works to the children of men! And let them sacrifice the sacrifices of thanksgiving, and declare his works with rejoicing (Psalm 107:8, 23).

The Clean Woman

The Clean Woman is one that has been violated during childhood and is now hiding behind her home.

Her home has become her castle and prison. She is constantly cleaning but it can never be clean enough. When you have been violated you never feel clean. This woman has become obsessed with cleanliness. No one can ever meet her expectations. She can never have a true friendship because she is suspicious of everyone. She brings this madness into her marriage and without healing her marriage will fail. When you bring unresolved problems into your marriage its not fair to your spouse because he will never understand your trauma until you are released from the bondage of your past.

She now has children and has projected the same spirit into her children without ever being healed. Every week it's new curtains or something new to change the setting of her castle.

When you create your own fortress you know exactly what it takes to keep you from going out of your environment. She finds excuses when its time to communicate with others or go to events and functions. Her husband becomes a loner and a prey for other women. She becomes addicted to alcohol and drugs because of her low self-esteem. She seeks for refuge in all the wrong places. Her heart cries out but only she alone can open the door of her heart to God. God came to heal the ones that are bruised and abused. As we come into Christ we accept Him but we hold onto the wounds of our past. We hide them while keeping busy doing things that are not producing fruit.

As we grow in Christ and the Word of God finds us we begin to rebuke the devil but its' not the devil but the dark side of you that needs to be redeemed. The dark side brings up the opposing thoughts of the past. God gave us His Word, "Let this mind be in you which was also in Christ Jesus: who being in the form of God, thought it not robbery to be equal with God" (Philippians 2:5-6). He said cast down imaginations and every high thing that exalteth itself against the knowledge of God, and bring into captivity every thought to the obedience of Christ (2nd Corinthians 10:5) we have been cleansed through the blood of Christ. When we receive the fountain of living water we can be made whole. For God so loved the world, that he gave his only begotten Son, that whosoever believe in him should not perish, but have everlasting life (John 3:16).

God has taken all our wounds and nailed them to a tree. But He was wounded for our transgressions, He was bruised for our iniquities: the chastisement of our peace was upon Him; and with His stripes we are healed (Isaiah 53:5).

Living Water: Behind every "Woman at the Well" there is a man waiting at home. When a woman lights up her home everything in it lights up. She is a mother, wife, homemaker, career woman and above all these she is God's woman because without Him she can do nothing (John 15:5). The woman that meets Jesus at the well is a woman of great experiences. Like the clean woman she also has many issues and needs for healing because she had five husbands and the one she has now was not her husband (John 4:18). The Bible does not expose her shame but lets us know that she possesses truth.

Jesus was sent there to release her from her bondages. When He has need of you He will loose you. She went to the well at noontime when the sun was the hottest. Her purpose was to avoid confrontation. Most women gossip when they get together and she did not want any conflict with her neighbors. Because of the offence brought to her by others. When you are not in the clique you have low-self esteem.

Each of us that are bruised by the system of men need to be affirmed. She was a no-name woman "but God who is rich in mercy,

Woman at the Well

for His great love wherewith He loved *us*" asked her for a drink, she was shocked that He had dignified her person." She said how is it that thou, being a Jew askest drink of me, which is a woman of Samaria? For the Jews have no dealings with the Samaritans. In the Hebrew writings the prime root for the Samaritans was to hedge about with thorns, in other words to guard, to protect, attend, beware and be circumspect, take heed to self. It was a watch station. Jesus answered and said unto her; if you knew the gift of God, and whom it is who says to you, give me a drink; you would have asked of Him, and He would have given thee living water (John 4:10).

    The woman said unto him, Sir, thou have nothing to draw with, and the well is deep. Where then do you get that living water? Are you greater than our father Jacob, who gave us the well, and drank from it himself? Jesus answered and said unto her, whosoever drink of this water will thirst again but whosoever drink of the water that I will give him shall never thirst, but the water I give him shall be in him a well of water springing up into everlasting life. The woman cried out sir give this water to drink but Jesus said unto her, call your husband and come here. The woman said I have no husband. Jesus said unto her, "You have well said, I have no husband, for you have had five husbands, and the one whom you now have is not your husband; in that you spoke truly." She then perceived that Jesus was a prophet (John 4:19). The woman began to talk about worship and how they worshipped in the mountains. Jesus said, *you know not* what you are worshipping. But my Father is looking for true worshippers that will worship the Father in spirit and in truth. God is a spirit they that worship him must worship him in spirit and truth (John 4: 24). She had heard that when the Messiah comes he would tell them all things. Then Jesus said unto her, "*I that speak am He.*" The woman left her water pots and fled to tell the men in the city. God wants us to be a witness to his coming.

His coming is very real as we see The Woman at the Well encountered at a time out of time. She had heard but now she can see. She was healed after she received the living water. It was so good and refreshing she wanted her neighbors to know. *"Come see a man, which told me all things that I ever did: is not this the Christ.* (John 4:29) She was loosed and set free because of the fountain of living water.

This woman represents the body of women that has been bruised by society. God came to set the captives free. Jesus said that "they that are whole need not a physician: but they that are sick" (Luke 5:31). There are many wells to drink from but there is only one well that has the living water.

Living Water: The law of the wise is a fountain of life, to depart from the snares of death (Proverbs 13:14). All the ways of a man are clean in his own eyes, but the Lord weighed the spirits (Proverbs 16:2).

The Gossip Woman

Sister Charlotte is a very prideful woman and had been divorced and left alone.

She is the A type personality that wants everything perfect. During the time of marriage she picked up a habit of drinking alcohol. She was very responsible and covered all her bases and only drank on the weekends. But her habits worsened and caused her husband to stay out late nights and sometimes for days.

When you are not happy you pick up habits. One of the habits was gossiping about people. She joined a church and tried to fit in the system of religion without being born again. When we have a filthy spirit and have not been saved you can hurt people and bring havoc into their life. The Bible tells us to "cleanse ourselves from all filthiness of the flesh and spirit, perfecting holiness in the fear of God" (2 Corinthians 7:1). Everyone that goes to church is not saved. She went to church with the wrong motives.

Sometimes we are so selfish in life that we can't see our wrong doings. She became friends with one of her sisters at church who learned her lifestyle and later talked about her to others. When you confide in people that means you trust them. The young woman told the stories about her past life before she was saved. When the young woman learned about her gossiping she went to another sister in church and prayed to God to forgive Sister Charlotte. She didn't take it to the pastor. The Bible says confess your faults one to another, and pray for one another, that ye may be healed. The effectual fervent prayer of a righteous man availeth much (James 5: 16). We thank God for the sister that didn't take the gossip to the pastor but was rooted in the word of God and released it as God said. He that covereth a transgression seeketh love; but he that repeateth a matter separateth very friends (Proverbs 17:9). Casting all your care upon him; for he careth for you (1 Peter 5:7).

After being in church for a while the Word of God pricked Sister Charlotte's heart and caused her to recognize her need for a Saviour. The church had an altar call and she went up and accepted Christ into her life. You can't be around the anointing of God and not get saved. "Evil communication corrupts good manners" (1 Corinthians 15:33). So good communication will produce good manners. Thank God for the fountain of living water that continue to add and multiply life to us.

Living Water: For by thy words thou shalt be justified, and by thy words thou shalt be condemned (Matthew 12:37).

The Jealous Woman

A Jealous Woman has no love for herself and she is never satisfied with herself. She always wants to be somebody else.

Her desires are the lust of the flesh, lust of the eyes and the pride of life, is not of the Father, but is of the world (1st John 2:16). In every community of life there are jealous women. As a whole body we can say that at one time or another we all have been jealous. This is a worldly spirit and if you were ever in the world you had this spirit. This spirit is much alive in our churches today.

If we are not called to carry a tune or sit on a committee we become envious. Each one of us has gifts and talents and some are greater than others. I heard T.D Jakes say, "If you begin to love who you are, you could never be jealous of anyone". Knowing who you are can make you alive. When God made you He created you individually different and gave each of us abilities to fulfill His promises. No one can do your job because he created you to do it. Each of us is uniquely made to God's specification. God didn't want you have a jealous spirit - that's why He said love one another as I have loved you (John 15:12). He repeated the commandment for us to love one another.

Love is not jealous. He that loves not knoweth not God, for God is love (1 John 4:8). There is no fear in love; but perfect love cast out fear: because fear hath torment. He that fear is not made perfect in love (1 John 4:18). This woman is in need of the fountain of living water that will speak to her spirit. Sometimes it takes patience to reach the essence of our soul. Jesus said, "The words He speaks are spirit and life" (John 6:63).

We are now back at the well where Jesus is speaking something that will bring life to the woman. *Whosoever drinketh of the water that I shall give him shall never thirst; but the water I shall give him shall be in him a well of water springing up into everlasting life*

(John 4:14). He is letting her know this water is everlasting. Now she is saying *O Lord thou hast searched me, and known me. Thou knowest my downsitting and mine uprising, thou understandest my thought afar off. Thou compassest my path and my lying down, and art acquainted with all my ways. For there is not a word in my tongue, but, lo, O Lord, thou knowest it altogether (Psalm 139: 1-4).* God is letting this woman know that He is all knowing and that He will be with her even if she makes her bed in hell. The spirit of jealousy will cause you to be suspicious and hinder you from receiving from God.

Living Water: Let all bitterness, and wrath, and anger, and clamor, and evil speaking, be put away from you, with all malice: and be ye kind one to another, tenderhearted, forgiving one another, even as God for Christ's sake hath forgiven you (Ephesians 4:31-32).

The Stone Woman
(single or married) Mark 12:19

The Stone Woman is wounded and damaged and has become beastly in her behavior. Her humanistic instincts are frozen in a defense mode similar to a guard. Suspicious by nature, she has a heart of unforgiveness and her brokenness has brought her to a suicide behavior. She has been programmed by the system of men to flow in society in a business or corporate world. She sustains her image by being deceitful. The corporate world has critically given her an inferior mindset so that she is unable to interact with family. God is not in her vocabulary and her mindset is like an animal that is roaming to find its way. Her words are "I deserve a good life with wealth and the finest of jewels...I work hard and I am not lazy...Why am I failing in my business...Why haven't I gotten married yet? I need help with the baby...Why does my family ignore me? They act as if I am not a part of them...I pray and God does not answer me."

Her husband leaves because of her negativity. He is not outgoing and he does not fit her lifestyle. She produces after her own kind. She weeps in the night from her cold heart and everything she touches turns to ice. She is hidden in religion and her heart is broken and her nights are sleepless. Her emotions are her covering.

God is the only one that can satisfy her. She is looking for a man that will satisfy her needs and every woman that looks for a man finds that her needs are not fulfilled in a man but in the purpose that God has called her for. God said, "Even every one that is called by My name: for I have created him for my glory, I have formed him; yea I have made him "(Isaiah 43:7). This woman was wounded in the house of her friends, those that she put her confidence in. And one shall say unto him, What are these wounds in thine hands? Then he shall answer, those with which I was wounded in the house of my friends.

(Zechariah 13:6). The word of God tells us to put no confidence in a friend (Micah 7:5).

    I will give them one heart, and I will put a new spirit within you: and I will take the stony heart out of their flesh, and give them a heart of flesh, that they may walk in my statutes, and keep mine ordinances, and do them and they shall be my people, and I will be their God (Ezekiel 11: 19-20). Just as the Woman at the Well, God has already prepared a day for deliverance; He will not allow us to stay in a state of rebellion. He is the Just One and nothing can pluck us out of his hand (John 10:29). The Stone Woman found justice in a merciful God.

    Living Water: Women are defined by society; in which they live in. Our environment has much to do with how we live and present ourselves. We live in a world that changes so fast that we are not able to keep up with technology. If you are not rooted and grounded in God you will be lost in the world. They wait on no one and everyone is in a hurry to get nowhere. The Bible states: that they that wait upon the Lord shall renew their strength; they shall mount up with wings as eagles; they shall run, and not be weary; and they shall walk, and not faint (Isaiah 40:31). Look at the fishes how they swim to and fro. They all have different sizes and shapes. But there is one thing they all have in common and that is they all need water. They cannot survive out of their environment. God (speaking) my people are out of my presence and they cannot survive without me. In my presence is fullness of joy (Psalms 16:11). There is righteousness and peace and joy in the Holy Ghost. Let these truths abide in your hearts.

The Women of Zion -Harps

The Women of Zion has hung their harps on the willow tree. The music has gone out of their lives and they have become hopeless.

Where are the women of Zion? How can we sing in a strange land? When you have been put into captivity and the trials of life have become such burdens you refuse to sing. God said make a joyful noise unto the Lord and serve the Lord with gladness and come before his presence with singing (Psalm 100:1-2). He also said "in every thing give thanks: for this is the will of God in Christ Jesus concerning you" (1Thessalonians 5:18). The harp means, "to celebrate the divine worship with music" (Hebrew Concordance).

God created us for His glory and all through the scripture he is letting us know our purpose. When He met The Woman at the Well He revealed to her about worship and how the Father seeks for us to worship Him in spirit and truth. The woman said to him, "our fathers worshipped in the mountains and you say Jerusalem is the place where men ought to worship. Jesus said unto her, Woman, believe me, the hour cometh, when you shall, neither in this mountain, nor yet at Jerusalem, worship the Father. But the hour cometh, and now is, when the true worshippers shall worship the Father in spirit and in truth: for the Father seeketh such to worship (John 4:19, 21, 23). The Psalms speaks to us about worship and praise and tells us how to praise and worship the Lord. Praise him with the sound of the trumpet: praise with the psaltery and harp. Praise him with the timbrel and dance: Praise him with stringed instruments and organs. Praise him upon the loud cymbals: praise him upon the high sounding, cymbals (Psalm 150:4-5). Sing unto him a new song; play skillfully with a loud noise (Psalm 33:3).

When the women of Zion begin to praise Him we will see the manifestation of God's glory. The husbands will return to their place in

God and the children's children will worship God in spirit and in truth. He said train the child while he is young and when he gets old he will not depart from the word. (Proverbs 22:6) And it shall come to pass afterward, that I will pour out my spirit upon all flesh; and your sons and your daughters shall prophesy, your old men shall dream dreams, and your young men shall see vision: And also upon the servants, and upon the handmaids in those days will I pour out my spirit (Joel: 2-28-29).

The women of Zion hung their harps on the willow tree because they were not recognized, and they were misunderstood because they were women of destiny. God has chosen instructors to bring about purpose in their lives. Now God has opened up many doors for women from all walks of life for His divine purpose. He said those who are first shall be last and those who are last shall be first (Mark 10:31). God said, "My people perish for lack of knowledge" (Hosea 4:6). For I am the Lord I do not change. (Malachi 3:6)

The women still have the message that says tell my brethren that they go into Galilee, and there shall they see me (Matthew 28:10). Galilee is considered the heathen circle that is a region in Palestine (Strong's Greek Concordance). This is a place of understanding. God said ask of Him and He would give us the heathen for our inheritance and the uttermost part of the earth for your possession (Psalm 2:8). The Woman At The Well left her water pot, and went her way into the city, and saith to the men, Come see a man, which told me all things that ever I did: is not this the Christ? They went out of the city, and came to him (John 4:28-29). She carried the message of life that brought life to others. When the sons of God are ready the teacher will appear.

Living Water: There is a spiritual journey we all must take and only God can reveal his Son to us. When we come into the knowledge of God we are babes that desire the sincere milk of the word (1 Peter 2:2). We look at the baby and see our level of understanding. Each baby is fed a different formula because some eat natural food and some of us eat a mixture. Each of us is different because we were taught differently, but some of the babes like a pacifier rather than milk. As we take this journey we will encounter many teachers but there is only one truth. Jesus said "Either make the tree good, and his fruit good; or else make the tree corrupt, and his fruit corrupt: for the tree is known by his fruit" (Matthew 12:33).

> *"The LORD is my light and my salvation— whom shall I fear? The LORD is the stronghold of my life—of whom shall I be afraid? (Psalm 27:1)*

Destiny

This woman of Destiny left her home to journey into another land. She left her family, which were her mother, father, her four children and husband. She talked with her family for many years before she finally made the decision to take her journey. She was a woman of destiny. Destiny reaches down into the soul of every person but some of us take heed and others never find their real purpose in life.

On the sixth day of creation God created man in his own image, in the image of God created he him; male and female created he them. And God blessed them, and God said unto them, be fruitful, and multiply, and replenish the earth, and subdue it: and have dominion over the fish of the sea and over the fowl of the air, and over every living thing that moveth upon the earth (Genesis 1:27-28). When you hear the call like Abraham did you don't need a confirmation because you have heard His voice that says "go and I will be with you." Abraham did not have a Bible to read and there was no prophet to prophesy over his life. But above all the other voices he ever heard this one was significant above them all and he gave God an eternal yes.

He left his fathers house to a land that he never knew. God said to him I will make you a great nation, and I will bless thee, and make thy name great; and thou shall be a blessing: And I will bless them that bless thee, and curse him that curseth thee: and in thee shall all families of the earth be blessed (Genesis 12:2-3). At that time Abraham had not a son for heir yet he believed that God would make him a great nation.

When God speaks, the impossible becomes possible, and we become fully persuaded. The Woman at the Well had destiny because God said "I must go to Samaria." (John 4:4) When God has need of you, He looses you to go. For He had purpose for the Samaritan woman and destiny awaited her. She became a messenger of light that would bring others to Christ. Jesus said if any man will come after Me, let him deny himself, and take up his cross daily, and follow me: For whosoever will save his life shall lose it: but whosoever will lose his life for My sake, the same shall save it (Luke 9: 23-24).

The woman that left everything for the glory of God has much to gain. Verily I say unto you, there is no man that hath left house, or brethren, or sisters, or father or mother, or wife, or children, or lands, for my sake, and the Gospels'. But he shall receive a hundredfold now in this time, houses, and brethren, and sisters, and mothers, and children, and lands, with persecutions; and in the world to come eternal life (Mark 10:29-30). As we said in the beginning destiny is for those who hear and obey the call.

Living Water: My word has purpose and it will accomplish where I send it. Don't fret about nothing just know that all things are working together for the good of those who love God and are called according to His purpose (Romans 8:28).

These are never ending stories because the woman will always need a drink from the well—the fountain of living water. Even though the women are in different cultures they are all women and when God met The Woman at the Well, she represented a need. We are creatures of need but "God shall supply all our need" according to his riches in glory by Christ Jesus (Philippians 4:19). We will continue our stories because maybe one might make a difference in your life.

Awesome Women of the Bible

> *"Trust in the LORD with all thine heart; and lean not unto thine own understanding. In all thy ways acknowledge him, and he shall direct thy paths."*
> *(Proverbs 3:5-6)*

Awesome Women of the Bible

Sarah

As we reflect back let us look at Sarah who is the mother of (nations) all living (Genesis 17:16).

Sarah was the wife of Abraham who conceived and brought forth a son in her old aged. But before her conception she brought forth many births with her travail. We have many women in the world, but to find one like Sarah is very few in number.

Sarah took her Egyptian maid Hagar and gave her to her husband Abraham to be his wife. He went into her and conceived and after the conception her mistress was despised in her eyes. After all she had been with Abraham for many nights and had gotten close.

When you don't wait on the Lord to work things out in your life, you will fall into bitterness. Sarah wanted her husband to have seed so she gave up her rights to a maid for a season. When you give up your rights sometimes you have to suffer the consequences.

The Lord visited Sarah and told her she shall bare a son in her old age and she laughed. And Sarah said, "God hath made me to laugh, so that all that hear will laugh with me" (Genesis 21:6). Hagar and Sarah lived in the same camp after the birth of Isaac. Sarah saw the son of Hagar mocking (that is being disrespectful) and she cried out to Abraham and said "Cast out this bondwoman and her son: for the son of the bondwoman shall not be heir with my son, *even* with Isaac" (Genesis 21:10). Earlier in the picture she asked the woman to lie with her husband and now she wanted her out. Abraham was grieved but God said unto him "hearken unto her voice; for in Isaac shall they seed be called (Genesis 21:12).

When we wait on the Lord, He makes all things work together for good to them that love God, to them who are called according to His purpose (Romans 8:28). Sarah was watchful and God favored her words. Sometimes our motives are not pure before God. Sarah's motive for having a son for her husband was pure in heart and God allowed them to make that choice but God already knew what his plan was for Sarah and Abraham.

Sarah is to be admired for her courage and stability during her wait for her promise. As you know when God promises something He will bring it to pass. God is faithful to His word. She was an awesome woman, but also needed to drink from the fountain of living waters. We all have issues that we can attest to but God has delivered us from them all through the blood of Christ. When you meet Him all things become new.

Living Water: But without faith it is impossible to please him: for he that come to God must believe that he is, and that he is a rewarder of them that diligently seek him (Hebrew 11:6). All the promises of God in him are yea, and in him Amen, unto the glory of God by us (2 Corinthians 1:20).

Esther

Esther is another woman that portrays an awesome part in the scripture. She is brought into a palace without her permission. Her destiny awaits her in the king's court and she is a virgin and very beautiful. She has been set-aside for such a time as this. The King is looking for a new queen because he dethroned Queen Vashti. And the king loved Esther above all the women, and she obtained grace and favour in his sight more than all the virgins; so he set the royal crown upon her head, and made her queen instead of Vashti (Esther 2:17).

During that time when you went before the king you had to be purified for twelve months. The days of purification was six months with oil of myrrh, and six months with sweet odors and with other things for purifying of women (Esther 2:12). God also prepares us to come into His presence in holiness. Esther had a divine call that will later be used to free her people from the hand of the enemy. Her enemy was a man called wicked Haman. He had plotted to slay the Jews. Mordecai was Esther's uncle who raised her in the absence of her parents. Mordecai saved the king's life and it was later recorded in the Book of Chronicles. (Esther 2:23).

Esther is our modern day woman who was placed into a position to help her people. God, through her uncle Mordecai charged her to make supplication for people to the king. Sometimes we are in a position to do the bidding for the Lord. Esther with brilliant beauty and excellent in charisma answered her uncle in this manner. Go, gather together all the Jews that are present in Shushan, and fast ye for me, and neither eat nor drink three days, night or day: I also and my maidens will fast likewise; and so will I go in unto the king, which is not according to the law: and if I perish, I perish (Esther 4:16). Esther had great courage and stood fast in her position to help her people.

When the king saw Esther the queen standing in the court, that she obtained favor in his sight: and the king held out to Esther the golden scepter that was in his hand. So Esther drew near and touched the top of the scepter (Esther5: 2). The law stated that whosoever come unto the king into the inner court, who is not called, there is one law of his to put him or her to death except the king holds out the golden scepter that he or she may live (Esther 4:11). Esther had not been called in thirty days. She used a petition to save her people and gained favor from the king. She portrayed great leadership.

There is no reference to God in the book of "Esther" but He is there in His people. The king granted Esther her petition, and the evil that was to destroy her people was reversed, and the Jews destroyed their enemies (Esther 7). The feast of Purim was to celebrate the Jews deliverance from genocide. Esther was awesome because she walked in obedience to God and she respected her position as queen and used her authority to influence the king. She fasted along with the people and had a spirit of humility. She denied herself and took up her daily cross and followed the way of the Lord.

Esther was an image of Christ who would come and lay down His life for his people.

Living Water: I am the good shepherd: the good shepherd gives his life for the sheep (John 10:11).

Ruth

Ruth is another woman that stands out in time of biblical history. She was a Moabitess that was predestined by God to marry into a Hebrew Family. Her virtuous spirit is to be commended because of the courage she had. When you lose all you have and have to start all over it takes courage to go forward.

Her husband and brother-in-law had died and also her father-in-law and only the two daughter-in-laws were left to care for the mother-in-law. Naomi said to her two daughter in-laws, go, and return each to her mother's house; the Lord deal kindly with you, as you have dealt with the dead, and with me (Ruth 1:8). Ruth was chosen to bring forth the promise of God. Her love and devotion for her mother-in-law Naomi was awesome. She takes her place as a daughter and said to Naomi entreat me not to leave you, or turn back from following after you; For wherever you go, I will go; And wherever you lodge, I will lodge; Your people shall be my people, And your God, my God. Where you die, I will die, and their will I be buried. The Lord do so to me, and more also If anything but death parts you and me (Ruth 1:16-17).

Ruth forsakes her land to go into a land unknown to her. Her faithfulness brought her to a wealthy place in God. Through her gleaning in the field of her kinsman Boaz she was able to make provision for her mother-in-law the widow and also through her marriage to Boaz a great king came through her loins - the Messiah (Matthew 1:5). She had a willing heart and a willing mind. This is an example of God's blessing on Ruth: "For the Lord your God is God of gods and Lord of lords, the great God, mighty and awesome, who shows no partiality nor takes a bribe. He administers justice for the fatherless and the widow, and loves the stranger, giving him food and clothing. Therefore love the stranger, for you were strangers in the land of Egypt" (Deuteronomy 10:17-19 NKJ). God is faithful to his word. Ruth earned respect and favor for her faithfulness.

Living Water: Who can find a virtuous woman? For her price is far above rubies (Proverbs 31:10).

Rahab

Rahab was an awesome woman who is one of the heroes of faith. She was willing to turn from her ways and the worship of idol gods to follow the God of Israel.

She had the courage, and the wisdom to hide the spies who sought out the land to destroy it. She had heard of the conquest of God's chosen people. As you know faith comes by hearing and hearing by the word of God (Romans 10:17). When she agreed to hide them she let them know she had heard how they had conquered the other nations that had been delivered from Egypt. Jericho was a walled city (Joshua 6:20).

Rahab asked for salvation for her and her household. "Now therefore I pray you, swear unto me by the Lord, since I have showed you kindness, that ye will also show kindness unto my father's house, and give me a true token" (Joshua 2:12). The spies let her know when they possess the land they will remember her. And the men answered her, our life for yours, if ye utter not this our business. And it shall be, when the Lord hath given us the land, that we will deal kindly and truly with thee" (Joshua 2:14).

She was instructed to let a red scarlet thread hang from her window so that they would not destroy them (Joshua 2:18). She was taken into the family of God through her faithfulness. "Joshua spared Rahab the harlot, her father's household, and all that she had.

So she dwells in Israel to this day, because she hid the messengers whom Joshua sent to spy out Jericho" (Joshua 6:25).

Living Water: Salvation belongs unto the Lord: thy blessing is upon thy people (Psalm 3:8). I, even I, am the Lord; and beside me there is no saviour (Isaiah 43:11).

> "Ye are the light of the world.
> A city that is set on a hill
> cannot be hid."
> *(Matthew 5:14)*

Lot's Wife

There are many awesome women in the Bible and there is one that we all can identify with and that is Lot's Wife. We as a body of women have all looked back at our past. The reflection of the past can destroy us if our heart is not sold out to God.

When God sent His angels to destroy Sodom and Gomorrah He said to Lot, "escape for thy life; look not behind thee" (Genesis 19:17). But his wife looked back from behind him, and she became a pillar of salt (Genesis 19:26). She was dissolved and became a barren land. A pillar is like a monument of something that is no longer mobilized. Jesus reminded us again in the New Testament about looking back. He said remember Lot's wife (Luke 17:32).

For Jesus to remind us of this woman is very significant. He leaves us with this: In that day, he which shall be upon the housetop, and his stuff in the house, let him not come down to take it away: and he that is in the field, let him likewise not return back (Luke 17:31). Sometimes what we possess becomes life to us but Jesus said, take heed, and beware of covetousness: for a man's life consisteth not in the abundance of the things, which he possesseth (Luke 12:15). Our lifestyle can be an idol in our temple if we don't give ourselves completely to God. Whatever we hold on to is what the enemy will destroy. When our life is committed to God then we have nothing to look back for.

Living Water: Paul gives us more to think about as he writes to the Philippians saying Brethren, I count not myself to have apprehended: but this one thing I do, forgetting those things which are behind, and reaching forth unto those things which are before, I press toward the mark for the prize of the high calling of God in Christ Jesus (Philippians 3:13-14). Therefore if any man be in Christ, he is a new creature: old things are passed away; behold, all things are become new (2 Corinthians 5:17). God has left us a witness, which was Lot's wife.

> *"For God hath not given us the spirit of fear; but of power, and of love, and of a sound mind."*
> *(2 Timothy 10:7)*

Hannah

Hannah represents the inner silence of a woman that is frustrated. She had everything she needed except a fruitful womb. She was married to a man that had two wives. She was one and the other was named Peninnah. Peninnah was fruitful but Hannah had no seed for her husband. When you are not producing you feel worthless.

Hannah's husband loved her more than the other wife and he gave Hannah a more worthy portion as they went yearly to worship and to sacrifice unto the Lord. Her husband sees her weeping and says to her, "why weepest thou? And why eatest thou not? And why is thy heart grieved? Am not I better to thee than ten sons?" (1 Samuel 1:8). During that time women who could not conceive thought themselves to be worthless. They felt honored to give birth.

Sometimes we are provoked to get the promise of God. The Bible tells us we have not because ye ask not (James 4:2). Peninah provoked Hannah to cry out in bitterness. The Bible states, "that she was in bitterness of soul, and prayed unto the Lord, and wept sore. And she vowed a vow, and said, O Lord of hosts, if thou will indeed look on the affliction of thine handmaid, and remember me, and not forget thine handmaid, but wilt give unto thine handmaid a man child, then I will give him unto the Lord all the days of his life, and there shall no razor come upon his head" (1 Samuel:9-11).

When she prayed she spoke in her heart only her lips moved and her voice was not heard and when Eli the priest saw Hannah praying he thought she was drunk but she responded "no my lord, I am a woman with a sorrowful heart." The priest answered and said "go in peace and the God of Israel will grant your request" (1 Samuel13-17).

Hannah conceived that she bare a son and called his name Samuel (1st Samuel 1:20). After he was weaned, Hannah took him to the priest. "For this child I prayed; and the Lord has given me my petition which I asked of him: Therefore also I have lent him to the Lord; as long as he Liveth he shall be lent to the Lord (1 Samuel 27-28).

The Lord visited Hannah, so that she conceived, and bare three sons and two daughters (1 Samuel 2:21). When you are willing to give something you love to the Lord he will "do exceeding abundantly above all that we ask or think, according to the power that worketh in us" (Ephesians 3:20). Hannah kept her promise to the Lord and her vow. To give your only child up to the Lord is an awesome thing; Hannah was rewarded with five children for her obedience. And Samuel grew, and the Lord was with him, and did let none of his words fall to the ground. And all Israel from Dan even to Beer-she-ba knew that Samuel was established to be a prophet of the Lord (1 Samuel 3:19-20).

Living Water: When we ask God to bless our womb who knows what greatness can come forth. For your shame you shall have double; and for confusion they shall rejoice in their portion: therefore in their land they shall possess the double: everlasting joy shall be unto them (Isaiah 61:7).

Mary

Mary, who is the mother of our Lord, is an awesome woman. God chose Mary for such a time as this. Mary was betrothed to Joseph in other terms engaged. According to the book of Luke, the angel Gabriel was sent from God unto a city of Galilee, named Nazareth, and the angel came unto her, and said Hail, thou art highly favored, the Lord is with thee: blessed art thou among women. And when she saw him, she was troubled at his sayings, and cast in her mind what manner of salutation this should be. And the angel said unto her, fear not, Mary: for thou hast found favor with God. And behold thou shalt conceive in thy womb, and bring forth a son, and shalt call his name JESUS. He shalt be great, and shall be called the Son of the Highest: and the Lord shall give him the throne of his father David: And he shall reign over the house of Jacob forever; and of his kingdom there shall be no end. Then Mary said how shall this be, seeing I know not a man? And the angel said unto her the Holy Ghost shall come upon thee, and the power of the Highest shall overshadow thee: therefore also that holy thing which shall be born of thee shall be called the Son of God. The angel let Mary know that her cousin Elizabeth hath also conceived a son in her old age, who was barren. *For with God nothing shall be impossible* (Luke 1:37). And Mary answered and "said behold the handmaid of the Lord; be it unto me according to thy word. Mary was so tuned into God that she did not need a confirmation but He let her know that Elizabeth was also chosen to bring forth in her old age, who was barren.

Sometimes when God tells us to do something we look for someone to confirm it. Mary received her call and purpose without considering Joseph, who she was engaged to. Her purpose for God was far greater than her betrothal to Joseph. In the Book of Matthew it tells how Joseph felt and how he responds to Mary being with Child before they came together. "Then Joseph her husband, being a just man, and not willing to make her a public example, was minded to put her away privily. But while he thought on these things, behold, the angel of the Lord appeared unto him in a dream, saying, Joseph thou son of David, fear not to take unto thee Mary thy wife: for that which is conceived in her is of the Holy Ghost" (Matthew 1:19-20). The same thing the angel said to Mary he said to Joseph. For our God is not the author of confusion, but of peace as in all churches of the saints (1 Corinthians14:33). Mary was chosen to carry the message just like the Woman at the Well.

Living Water: Let's remember, "many are called but few are chosen" (Matthew 20:16). Lo, children are an heritage of the Lord and "the fruit of the womb is His reward (Psalm 127:3). Mary was a woman that drank from the fountain of living water.

These women are messengers for all generations that we may be fully persuaded that we have need of a Savior. The Woman at the Well is still carrying the message.

Seasons of Life

> *"But without faith it is impossible to please him: for he that cometh to God must believe that he is, and that he is a rewarder of them that diligently seek him."*
> *(Hebrews 11:6)*

Seasons of Life

Josephine

Josephine is a woman that is young and full of energy and her life is bubbling. She loves life with a passion and her goals are to become an actress and make lots of money. Josephine represents all who are blinded by the enemy. Silly Women: *For this sort are they, which creep into houses, and lead captive silly women laden with sins, led away with divers lusts (2 Timothy 3:6).*

Sometimes our own selfish desires cause us not to see truth and we fall prey to the devil. The Bible tells us if we delight ourselves in the Lord: and he shall give thee the desires of thine heart" (Psalm 37:4). One day she met a nice man and began to date. They dated for about six months and decided to have pre-marital sex and as a result Josephine got pregnant. Her life began to take a turn for the worse. She found out that the man she had been dating had a wife in another state. This was a devastating experience. After all she had wanted a career in acting. Before laying down our life we need to know our purpose in life, and also the person we will be spending it with. Afterwards, Josephine purposed in her heart to keep the child then the father of the child said he was going to get a divorce.

If a man leaves his wife for one woman he would leave again for another woman. Josephine told her family and they rejected her and then she began to be bitter. One day she met a woman who had experienced the same in her relationship. The stranger let her know that she also had a baby but didn't know she was pregnant until it was time for the baby to arrive. She was a Christian woman that had given of herself and decided that the man she was dating was unequally yoked with her so she dismissed him and said she never wanted to see him again. Later about six months she went into labor not knowing she had conceived. She had no prenatal care all during her pregnancy. She let Josephine know that God was showing her what was done in the dark was brought to the light. The bible tells us that all things that are reproved are made manifest by the light: for whatsoever doth make manifest is light (Ephesians 5:13). But if we walk in the light, as he is in the light, we have fellowship one with another, and the blood of Jesus Christ his Son cleanseth us from all sin (1ˢᵗ John 1:7). Josephine needed to be saved. The stranger led her to the Lord with her testimony. Josephine repented and received Christ Jesus in her life. She found out that she was not the only one that had sinned and come short of the glory of God (Romans 3:23). Knowing truth can set you free.

The Woman at the Well found truth and left her water pots to spread the good news. Josephine is one of many that have need of a Savior.

Living Water: I will never leave you nor forsake you (Hebrews 13:5). Walk in my word and truth will be established. Let not your heart be troubled about anything (John 14:1). Count not your life dear to you; your life is hid with Christ in God (Colossians 3:3). Walk in the light and you will be called the children of light (John 12:36). All my promises are yes and Amen (2 Corinthians 1:20).

Lukewarm

Lukewarm woman is a woman that mixes a lie with faith and she changes from day to day. One day she is on fire for the Lord and the next day she is trouble. She is neither hot nor cold (Revelation 3:15-16). She hides in the cloak of religion. For unto us was the Gospel preached, as well as unto them: but the word preached did not profit them, not being mixed with faith in them that heard it (Hebrew 4:2). A lie and the truth can't mix because it will cause the bread to be polluted. Doubt and unbelief can't stand. He that comes to God must believe that He is God and He is a rewarder of them that diligently seek Him (Hebrews 11:6).

She has a form of godliness but denies the power within (2 Timothy 3:5). Lukewarm women are deceptive and think more highly of themselves then they should. She is critical about everybody and her goal is to have the best of both worlds. When its time to make a decision they are skeptical and they look for confirmations and affirmations. She is always looking for a word from the Lord and has not been obedient to the last word she heard. When you confront her with truth she says "I am not there yet or I am in a different place." The Bible tells us that we are forever learning and never come into the knowledge of truth (2 Timothy 3:7). She is a woman that has not found her purpose. The Bible tells us to seek first the kingdom of God and his righteousness; and all these things shall be added (Matthew 6:33). The only way the Woman at the Well received her promise was to have an encounter with the Lord. She had things in her life that needed to be answered.

Jesus made known to the Woman at the Well whom He was and what He had to offer. He let her know that the water from the well will cause her to thirst again "but whosoever drinketh of the water that I shall give him shall never thirst; but the water that I shall give him shall be in him a well of water springing up into everlasting life." She said to him "Sir, give me this water, that I thirst not, neither come hither to draw. He said to her "go call thy husband, and come hither she said, "I have no husband.'" He said to her you have had five husbands; and whom thou now have is not your husband." She then perceived that he was a prophet (John 4:15-19).

God is the only one that speaks to your person and gender and tells your life story. When the truth is revealed that's when the woman became loose from the bondage in her life and she left her water pots to tell others that she found a man that told her everything about herself. The Lukewarm Woman was such as this that needed to be introduced to Jesus. She is no longer confused about the coming Messiah because she has been introduced to Him. When you have not been properly introduced to your Father you wonder and are always looking for someone to confirm your action. She found life at the well - so will all who desire the Living Water.

Living Water: And unto the angel of the church of the Laodiceans write; These things saith the Amen, the faithful and true witness, the beginning of the creation of God; I know thy works, that thou art neither cold nor hot: I would thou wert cold or hot. So because thou art lukewarm, and neither cold nor hot, I will spew thee out of my mouth. Because thou sayest, I am rich, and increased with goods, and have need of nothing; and knowest not that thou art wretched and miserable, and poor, and blind, and naked (Revelation 3:14-17). If any of you lack wisdom, let him ask of God, that giveth to all men liberally, and upbraideth not; and it shall be given him. But let him ask in faith, nothing wavering. For he that wavereth is like a wave of the sea driven with the wind and tossed. For let not that man think that he shall receive anything of the Lord. A double-minded man is unstable in all his ways (James 1: 5-8).

Woman of Issues

A Woman of issues is one that has been broken and beaten down and crushed for the Master's use. As you know in order to get the oil from the olive it has to be crushed. There are many women in today's society that have been brought to this place of blessing. The Woman with the Issue of Blood had her issue for twelve years. During these twelve years the bible said she spent her living on many physicians (Mark 5:26). When you have issues you look for help in all the wrong places. But when she heard of Jesus she came into the press behind him and touched His garments. For she said, "If I may touch His clothes, I shall be whole." And straightway the fountain of her blood was dried up; and she felt in her body that she was healed of that plague (Mark 5:27-29). This woman pressed her way into the Kingdom with everything trying to keep her out. Her inner silence was so great that when she touched Jesus, virtue went out of Him. He responded to her faith and he said unto her, "Daughter, thy faith hath made thee whole; go in peace, and be whole of thy plague" (Mark 5:30,34).

Sometimes our issues come from unforgiveness. The body responds to our thoughts. The Bible tells us to lay hands suddenly on no man, neither be partaker of other men's sins: keep thyself pure (1 Timothy 5:22). Shedding innocent blood can cause us to have disease from the words we speak. And the tongue is a fire, a world of iniquity: so is the tongue among our members, that it defileth the whole body (James 3:5-6).

When Jesus asked, "who touched my clothes?" The woman fearing and trembling, knowing what was done in her, came and fell down before him, and told him all the truth (Mark 5:30, 33). Only the truth can set us free, and that's what the woman at the well confessed was the truth.

Woman at the Well

"Jesus said unto her, go call thy husband, and come hither." The woman answered and said, "I have no husband." Jesus said unto her, thou hast well said, I have no husband. For thou hast had five husbands; and he whom thou now hast is not thy husband: in that saidst thou truly (John 4:16-18).

There are many women today with issues as this woman had who are fighting different types of disease in their bodies. We are to "let all bitterness, and wrath, and anger, and clamour, and evil speaking, be put away from us with all malice (Ephesians 4:31) But speak the truth in love, that you may grow up into him in all things, which is the head, even Christ (Ephesians 4:15). And be ye kind one to another, tenderhearted, forgiving one another, even as God for Christ's sake hath forgiven you (Ephesians 4:32). I believe this woman received the new man, which after God is created in righteousness and true holiness.

Jesus met the Woman at the Well, which had many issues, and He spoke to her person, gender, and her spirit and let her know about the Living Water. He knew about her lifestyle. He poured so much love into her that she left her water pots to tell the others in her city (John 4:28).

Living Water: Brethren, if any of you do err from the truth, and one convert him; Let him know, that he which converted the sinner from the error of his way shall save a soul from death, and shall hide a multitude of sins (James 5: 19-20).

Woman at the Well

Bread Winner (wives)

Every wise woman builds her house; but the foolish pluck it down with their hands (Proverbs 14:1). God has poured out his unfailing mercy to his daughters and sons. We who have had the opportunity to be the only one bringing in the provisions have lived in denial about our husbands. We will talk about the familiar to break the bands of wickedness. The house of the wicked shall be overthrown: but the tabernacle of the upright shall flourish (Proverbs 14:11).

There was a woman who had worked 12 years in the library and her husband had been working on his job for 22 years but he only brought home two hundred dollars. This woman didn't get to see a pay stub in all those years. As you know some of us are married for conveniences and some of us are one in the spirit. God joined us together to be one unit.

This woman's husband was on drugs but she lived in denial of his habit. The type of work he did was under the table so she had no check stub to base her conviction. Some of our husbands are womanizers, watch pornography, overeaters, alcoholics, and unbelievers. These are just a few that we can identify with. We are to pay attention to our husbands and their life styles to make sure it has the family interest. When we neglect the home our house becomes a shamble.

Women can be prideful when they are bringing in the most bread. When our house is out of order our children become undisciplined. We as parents are the only light that the child sees. If our light becomes dim then the children suffer for our lack of parenthood. One day this woman called a woman of God to rescue her from this destruction. The woman of God built up her low self-esteem and encouraged her to better her condition. She responded to her in this manner: "You need to re-establish your life by opening up a bank account."

Woman at the Well

She needed housing and all her checks from her previous accounts had insufficient funds. (God is a present help in time of trouble. – Psalm 46:1). In order for her to do business she needed a bank account. The woman of God took her to the bank where she did her business. The bank refused to give her an account unless she was a family member. The woman of God said "she is my sister" but they did not believe her because she was a woman of color. She referred to her as sister because they had the same Father, which is God. Without further misunderstanding they agreed to give her the account. "If God be for you who can be against you?" (Romans 8:31).

The woman's self-esteem was so low that her children were difficult to handle. The woman of God took her to a recreation center so that her kids would have an outlet to be with other children in an environment that was better controlled. When she got to the center, they responded to her that the center was booked up. The woman of God took it to another level by contacting the director of the recreation center. The director over-rode the first answer and her children were given permission to be a part of the recreation center. The story is not over yet, there is more.

It was now Wednesday night - everything started in the beginning of the week. The woman of God asked her to go to church and she said "I will pray and ask God about Sunday." On Sunday she was obedient and went to church. When she went up to put in her offering the man of God stopped her and said, "I am led by God to give you the money that was taken up in all three services." She was in awe. They did not give it to her that day but they sent her a check.

God is faithful when we are walking in obedience. He said if we be willing and obedient we can eat the good of the land (Isaiah 1:19). The woman of God was a well that met the needs of a stranger. Her marriage has been reconciled and they have moved to another state. Like the woman at the well she needed a drink from the fountain of living waters. Remember, the Good Shepherd laid down His life for the sheep (John 10:11).

Living Water: Submitting yourselves one to another in the fear of God. Wives, submit yourselves unto your own husbands, as unto the Lord. For the husband is the head of the wife, even as Christ is the head of the church: and He is the saviour of the body. Therefore as the church is subject unto Christ, so let the wives be to their own husbands in everything. Husbands love your wives, even as Christ also loved the church, and gave Himself for it (Ephesians 5:21-25).

> *"Be ye therefore followers of God, as dear children; And walk in love, as Christ also hath loved us, and hath given himself for us an offering and a sacrifice to God for a sweetsmelling savour."*
> *(Ephesians 5:1-2)*

Alabaster Box

The alabaster box represents what is precious in our hearts and holds the treasure of life in each of us. The woman that poured her most valuable possession into Jesus gave up her life to embrace him. For her ointment was precious to her. She was a woman who had heard about Jesus and sought him out and found him in the house of Simon the leper (Matthew 26:6).

The Bible tells us "there came a woman having an alabaster box of very precious ointment, and poured it on his head, as he sat at meat. But, when his disciples saw it, they had indignation, saying, to what purpose is this waste for this ointment might have been sold for much and given to the poor. When Jesus understood it, he said unto them, why trouble the woman for she hath wrought a good work upon me." Jesus said, "ye have the poor always with you; but me ye have not always. For in that she hath poured this ointment on my body, she did it for my burial" (Matthew 26:6-12).

Women love to smell good but if there is sin in our lives perfume will not cover it up. She poured into Christ and in return she received eternal life. He gave her a lifetime memorial for her gift. He said, "Verily I say unto you, wheresoever this gospel shall be preached in the whole world, there shall also this, that this woman hath done, be told for a memorial of her (Matthew 26:13).

She poured all she had into the Lord just as the widow woman. And he called unto him his disciples, and saith unto them, "Verily I say unto you, that this poor widow hast cast more in, than all they which have cast into treasury: For all they did cast in of their abundance; but she of her want did cast in all that she had, even all her living" (Mark 12:43-44).

When you give your best in worship God pours back into you, "pressed down, shaken together, running over, shall men pour back into your bosom. For with the same measure that ye mete withal it shall be measured to you again" (Luke 6:38).

The woman with the alabaster box worshipped God and stood at His feet behind Him weeping, and began to wash His feet with her tears, and did wipe them with the hairs of her head, and kissed his feet, and anointed them with ointment (Luke 7:38-39). The Bible tells us to humble ourselves under the mighty hand of God, that He may exalt you in due time (1st Peter 5:6). She had a revelation of His love and reverenced Him in humility. (When you have been looking for love in all the wrong places and finally find it, you sell all that you have to buy this great treasure which is like the kingdom of heaven seeking for goodly pearls who when he had found one pearl of great price went out and sold all that he had, and bought it (Matthew 13:45-46).

Her perfume was precious so she gave a worthy offering. She gave a willing offering. Sometimes God fights with us to get us into our place. But when you are willing and obedient you get to eat the good of the land (Isaiah 1:19). Jesus felt the love coming from her spirit because she had watered His feet with her tears and wiped them with her hair and anointed his head with oil. Jesus said, "wherefore I say unto thee, her sins, which are many, are forgiven; for she loved much: but to whom little is forgiven, the same loveth little (Luke 7:47). Like The Woman at the Well she left her water pots to tell the story. When we give up our desire, then Christ in us, the hope of glory can be fulfilled (Colossians 1:27). John said, "I must decrease so he can increase (John 3:30).

Living Water: Forever O Lord thy word is settled in heaven and thy faithfulness is every morning. I will ride upon the circle of the earth and what I have purposed shall come to pass. My word will stand forever and will accomplish where I send it. Walk in My divine nature and give no provision to the flesh. The spirit is willing but the flesh is weak. Remember, the wind as *it* blows and you know not where it comes from, so is my Holy Spirit to those that have been born of the spirit. (Psalm 119:89, 90), (Isaiah 55:11), (Matthew 26:41), (John 3:8). But we have this treasure in earthen vessels that the excellency of the power may be of God, and not of us (2 Corinthians 4:7). For where your treasure is there will your heart be also (Matthew 6:21).

> "Ye have not chosen me, but I have chosen you, and ordained you, that ye should go and bring forth fruit, and that your fruit should remain: that whatsoever ye shall ask of the Father in my name, he may give it you."
> *(John 15:16)*

Water Your Marriage

Marriage is divinely appointed by God and for God. The only way marriage can be successful is to be in Christ. God said how can two walk together unless they agree (Amos 3:3). It all starts with a disagreement. Negative words can cause contention in a marriage. When you are not being consistent it can cause you to focus elsewhere.

But our conception has been played out in another scene. Each role has its purpose to fulfill things God called us to do. When a man becomes passive he has lost something that he thought he had control over. It could be his masculinity, sickness, a job, a friend, or some other addiction that caused him to not care about his disposition. The way you carry yourself speaks loud and clear.

We as women need to pay attention to all signs of neglect. Servitude starts at home. Listen carefully and attentive and look for the good qualities of your mate. Let your motives be pure. Write out your painful emotions and give them to God and focus where you want to be.

There are times when we neglect one another with our busy schedule. Harmful words come from not being watered with the Word. God said meditate on the word day and night so that you can prosper (Psalm 1:2). Prosperity is a product of your spirit. The word of God tells us that "Beloved, I wish above all things that thou mayest prosper and be in health, even as thy soul prospereth" (3 John 2).

The Woman at the Well had five husbands and the one she had now was not her husband. Jesus met her there to give her a drink from the fountain of living water. Water of life purifies our souls. The natural water that we drink is also a cleanser. God's word is water. When we drink this water we are able to pour into others what He has freely given to us. What's contained in love is respect for one another.

Living Water: *This is my commandment, that you love one another,* as I have loved you (John 15:12).Submitting yourselves one to another in the fear of God. Wives, submit yourselves unto your own husbands, as unto the Lord. For the husband is the head of the wife, even as Christ is the head of the church: and He is the saviour of the body. Husbands, love your wives, even as Christ also loved the church, and gave himself for it; That he might sanctify and cleanse it with the washing of water by the word (Ephesians 5:21-26).

Spiritually Bankrupt

This is a woman that is spiritually bankrupt. She is out of energy, out of the Word, has lost her bearing and unable to discern right from wrong. She was looking for love in all the wrong places.

Sometimes we look for love in a marriage, in careers, and in friendship but we fail to "seek ye first the kingdom of God in his righteousness and all these things will be added" (Matthew 6:33). The Woman at the Well was waiting for the Messiah in her heart. She knew that when He comes He would reveal all things to her.

We can become spiritually bankrupt listening to the messenger of Satan that can never free you from bondage but bring your thoughts into servitude; "As a man think in his heart so is he." (Proverbs 23:7). But God in His infinite wisdom said to His Son Jesus," I must need to go to Samaria" (John 4:4). When God has need of something, He looses it for His purpose. The woman that was bowed down for eighteen years He loosed because she represented the promise. He said "ought not this woman being a daughter of Abraham whom Satan hath bound, lo these eighteen years, be loosed from this bond on the Sabbath (Luke 13:16)? This infirmity had her bowed down and could in no wise lift up herself. And when Jesus saw her, he called her to him, and said unto her, *Woman, thou art loosed from thine infirmity* (Luke 13:11-12).

Only God knew the condition of her soul and he spoke to her spirit and she heard and was lifted up. Only God can dignify our person. Like The Woman at the Well His words brought life to her spirit. Sometimes words of defeat can bow us down with weights. Take heed to what you hear.

Living Water: The Bible tells us that, "This book of the law shall not depart out of thy mouth; but thou shalt meditate therein day and night, that thou mayest observe to do according to all that is written therein: for then thou shalt make thy way prosperous, and then thou shalt have good success" (Joshua 1:8). As the living Father hath sent Me, and I live by the Father: so he that eateth Me, even He shall live by Me" (John 6:57). The Woman At The well is never ending but whosoever drinketh of the water that I shall give him shall never thirst; but the water that I shall give him shall be in him a well of water springing up into everlasting life" (John 4:14). When God fills you, you will never be spiritually bankrupt. Praise Him for He is worthy.

Cluttered Soul

This soul is cluttered with earthly possessions; shoes, pocket books, dresses, hats, dishes, ornaments, careers and our own ideology. This woman has her own agenda and has purpose in her heart to make it work without the will of God. God's will is in His Word and out of the Word is out of the will of God.

When we begin to pursue our careers and do our own thing without the leadership of the Holy Spirit, our soul becomes cluttered. We receive the spirit of delusion because of our multifaceted attitudes. The Bible tells us without Him we can do nothing (John 15:5). This woman wants both of the two worlds. In Christ we give up the world and walk in the spirit so we will not fulfill lusts of the flesh. The flesh mind is the enemy against God for it will not be subject to the law of God neither indeed can be, and so that they that are in the flesh cannot please God (Romans 8:7-8).

A cluttered soul wants a lot of things around them to draw attention to themselves. They need things such as knowledge and gifts to draw attention and people to them. They try to buy friendships and allow themselves to be used and manipulated. *needs a fix*

They are in relationships that hold them captive by diminishing and demising their self-esteem and telling them that they are not worthy to be liked by anyone but them. This soul has been paralyzed and is unable to function in society without co-dependency. They always feel that they need to be with someone. They cannot function alone. They are constantly seeking for company. When you look for love in all the wrong places you will soon find the match and if you light it, the enemy is there to destroy it. The thief cometh not, but for to steal, and kill, and to destroy: But God comes "that we might have life, and that we might have it more abundantly" (John 10:10).

Woman at the Well

We know that by the Word, The Woman at the Well had five husbands and the one she had now was not her husband. We know that she had a cluttered soul because of her lifestyle, but God who is rich in mercy stopped by to release her from the bondage of men. In her heart she was waiting on Jesus because she said, "when Messias comes, which is called Christ he will tell us all things. Jesus saith unto her, I that speak unto to thee am He "(John 4:25-26). Jesus did not judge her by her outward life but He saw her heart. God had given him a quick understanding in the fear of the Lord: "and he shall not judge after the sight of His eyes, neither reprove after the hearing of his ears" (Isaiah 11:3). We thank God for The Woman at the Well because we know that there is hope for the generations to come. He is that Bread of Life that came down from heaven that we may eat and not die (John 6:50).

Living Water: The Lord is in His holy temple let all the earth keep silent before Him (Habakkuk 2:20). He has cleansed us and washed us with His blood. The light of His glory will shine through us and dispel all darkness. Put on the new man, which has been renewed in righteousness and true holiness (Ephesians 4:23-24). Walk in submission and surrender to the will of God. We are His workmanship created in Christ Jesus unto good works, which God hath before ordained that we should walk in them (Ephesians 2:10). We are the branches and without the True Vine we can do nothing (John 15:1, 5). The truth is the only thing that will keep us free from the bondage of men. Today, walk in a knowing and you will be an expression of His glory and all those who look upon you will know that you are His. Walk in truth and truth will sustain you. Love all people.

Silent Frustration

This story tells us about a woman in her silence who has been rejected by her husband, because she received her destiny call from God. God calls us into a place with him that we cannot refuse. He makes the rough way smooth and the crooked road straight (Luke 3:5).

When your husband disagrees with your calling it causes jealousy and resentment. This woman retired from her job and started her own business and it is now flourishing but her marriage is bitter and cruel. As a result of this change in her life her husband started to drink and separate himself from her. His words are negative against her.

Every time a prophet comes to her church, they tell her about her situation. She listens and praises the Lord with a high praise. She has made up her mind to stand against the wile of the enemy. Her character is graceful and full of peace but her inner silence is like Hannah's, so she lays her tears before God. Her silence has caused some of the religious spectators to be concerned. God has promised her the ministry with her husband and He cannot lie.

Let us not forget the call on Abraham's life when God told him to leave his father's house. When God called Abraham he believed the spoken word. "And we know that all things work together for good to them that love God, to them who are called according to his purpose" (Romans 8:28). This woman has stepped up to the plate and is willing to hold the fortress. Her husband wants a divorce but her heart is still holding fast to God's promise. When you are going through silent frustration you have to get alone and scream and release the disappointments. As we know there is a water relief for every situation. The Woman at the Well was relieved after she received the word from the living God. A word in due season can set you free (Proverbs 15:23).

Living Water: Cast not away therefore your confidence, which hath great recompense of reward. For you have need of patience, that, after you have done the will of God, you might receive the promise. (Hebrews 10:35-36).

Love Bug

The love bug brings you back to the story of the woman with the Alabaster Box. In comparison, this woman's love was rejected by men but not by Jesus (Mark 14:4-9). When mankind rejects love you need to pour it into a vessel.

This woman has been beaten as a child and violated. Her tendency to love comes from all the rejections and disappointments in life. Sometimes our parents' die leaving us with the responsibility of our siblings but God said, "when my mother and father forsake me, then the Lord will take me up" (Psalm 27:10). When you have been left to bear the burdens of life you find a way to release the love that has been rejected. When opportunity presents itself you begin to pour into those that will receive. Most people run from you because they cannot believe that love has no motive but love. "Love is longsuffering, kind, its not jealous, is not boastful, not arrogant, not rude, not selfish, not resentful, does not think evil, rejoices in the truth, bears all things, believe all things, hope all things and endure all things"(1 Corinthians 13).

When you meet women who are willing to pour out of themselves with a hug that means they also want to receive a hug. There is no gender when it comes down to love because women and men alike portray this pattern. This is called related love. "For God so loved the world, that he gave his only begotten Son, that whosoever believe in him should not perish, but have everlasting life" (John 3:16).

Living Water: This is my commandment, that you love one another, as I have loved you (John 15:12). You have not chosen me, but I have chosen you, and ordained you, that you should go and bring forth fruit, and that your fruit should remain: that whatsoever you shall ask of the Father in My name, He may give it to you (John15: 16). If the world hates you, you know that it hated Me before it hated you (John 15:18).

> *"He that loveth not knoweth not God; for God is love."*
> *(1 John 4:8)*

Vashti (Conceited Woman)

Vashti is a woman but can also be a male who is self-righteous and deceitful against God's will, and thinks she or he cannot be replaced. This is a competitive spirit seeking power. She comes to discourage the bakers in Christ. She comes when everything is working smoothly so she can see what happen. The Bible tells us blessed is the man that walketh not in the counsel of the ungodly, nor standeth in the way of sinners, nor sitteth in the seat of the scornful (Psalm 1:1). She is very offensive and becomes very prideful when she is asked of her husband to submit. She does not walk in humility or submission yet knows the definition, but refuses. She is arrogant and has confidence in her own ability. This is what is called a self-governing spirit.

As we look at her character we can see that she has no morals. Her behavior is one that shames her husband. According to the book of Esther queen Vashti refused to come at the king's commandment by his chamberlains: therefore was the king very wroth, and his anger burned in him (Esther 1:12). We as wives are to obey our husbands. When we walk in disobedience we cause other women to do likewise.

Husband is the head of the wife, even as Christ is the head of the church: and he is the saviour of the body (Ephesians 5:22-23). Husbands, love your wives, even as Christ also loved the church, and gave himself for it; that he might sanctify and cleanse it with the washing of water by the word, that he might present it to himself a glorious church, not having spot, or wrinkle, or any such thing; but that it should be holy and without blemish (Ephesians 5:25-27). Vashti's spirit is a controlling spirit that uses her power as the queen to take over but God has set the stage for her and all her props will be taken down. The king made a law for all women because of this one woman that did not reverence her husband. The Bible tells us that because of this deed of the queen shall come abroad unto all women, so that they shall despise their husbands in their eyes, when it shall be reported, the king Ahasuerus commanded Vashti the queen to be brought in before him, but she came not (Esther 1:17). Because the queen refuse to show her beauty to the people before the king he made a "royal commandment and said let it be written among the laws of the Persians and Medes, that it be not altered, That Vasthi come no more before the king and let the king give her royal estate unto another that is better than she" (Esther 1:19).

When we become so high minded that we can't be moved, God can bring down as He sit up (Psalm 75:7). For, "He resist the proud but give grace to the humble" (1 Peter 5:5). This woman represents a church that has been disobedient to her king. That Vashti come no more before the king and let the king give her royal estate unto another that is better than she" (Esther 1:19).

Living Water: Nevertheless let every one of you in particular so love his wife even as himself; and the wife see that she reverence her husband (Ephesians 5:33). A new commandment I give unto you, that you love one another; as I have loved you, that ye also love one another. By this shall all men know that you are my disciples, if you have love one to another.

The Woman Left Desolate

There are many women who put their entire life on hold for their children. When you are a single mom raising your child you forget about sharing your life with another person. One day the son or daughter grows up and gets married and leaves home. You begin to look across the table or look into your extra bedroom or you overcook. When you finally discover that you are left desolate you make calls to your children often. This can cause jealousy in a marriage. When a mother-in-law checks too often it can cause strife and contention. Your emotions grab hold of you and you realize that he or she is gone to share his or her life with someone else.

The Bible tells us that "a man shall leave his father and his mother, and shall cleave unto his wife: and they shall be one flesh" (Genesis 2:24). The woman with the only son has put everything into him and now finds herself desolate and lonely. She is fearful of getting married because her past has not been forgiven. She becomes a Eunuch by choice and lives a life of celibacy. Her career is her only friend and her nights are spent weeping. She needs a well, but her pride keeps her comfortable.

She refused to have a relationship that will cause her to be committed. When you are not committed to someone you will fall into something. The Woman at the Well was lonely. But when she met Jesus and He spoke to her person and told her all she ever did, she left her water pots and fled to tell the story. Jesus is waiting at the well for all those who need a drink. The well satisfies our needs and removes loneliness. The water gives us a testimony that will never quench our thirst.

Living Water: After you have been purged and accepted the Beloved you should have no more consciousness of sin (Hebrew

10:2). "I have redeemed you and I remember your sins no more from the 'East to the West,' I have forgotten (Psalms 103:12). He that is born of God cannot sin because my seed remain in you. (1st. John 3:9)." Let peace have her perfect work. Peace is the empire of your soul. If it be possible, as much as lie in you, live peaceable with all men; without it you cannot see God (Romans 12:18).

We are blessed because we are the peacemakers (Matthew 5:9). Trust me to walk in you. For I have set you aside for such a time as this. I have given to you life more abundantly and now go and give it to others. Go, and I will be with you.

Grieving Women

These women have been violated in society by relationships, families, and jobs and loved ones and have lost their strength to follow on to their destiny.

These women shut down their hearing, seeing and understanding. They are like a leaky faucet that drips and has no flow. These women have a reprobate mind because they have left their first love by leaning on their own understanding. "There is a way that seems right in every man's eye but the way is separation and destruction (Proverbs 16:2)."

They are always seeking others ideas that are not ideas for them. They have been broken and are looking back at their past and is afraid of their future. Their circumstances have caused them to doubt the things God has told them.

One woman lost her mom and grieved for three years. Her husband didn't know it and her family didn't conceive it but her pain was locked up in her soul. Her mother was her best friend and when she left part of her went too. She tries to face life without being exposed but a well comes into her life. A well is one that has the flowing water of life coming up out of her belly. Only a well can relieve you from the wounds of life. This is a job for Jesus.

This woman was made well when she was confronted with what she was carrying in her soul. She was tied to her mother's soul. Her mother had become an idol in her temple. When you put something before God it becomes an idol. He said put no images before Him. After being exposed she cried out so loud that you could hear the grief leaving her soul. Afterward she released her mother back to God and was healed immediately. We thank God for the well that never runs dry that continually flows with mercy and truth.

Another woman was grieving because she could not find her destiny. She looked in all the places that she could imagine. Her careers were her hope for life. She wanted to make money and have a lovely life with a husband and children. She became celibate for a season. Every man she dated left her desolate and her family rejected her. She grieved after the lost of her mother at an early age. She practices religion until she met a well and accepted Christ as her personal Savior. After accepting the Lord she studied the Bible for about three years and was happy in the Lord until she met her dream.

Her dream was a man that she wanted to be her husband. Sometimes we have our own agenda for our lives. It only takes one thought to change your life forever. She left her studies and went after her destiny and about five years later she became angry because things were not working out the way she planned in her mind. Sometimes we plan things and expect them to be God's plan for our lives. She is angry because he only sees her as a friend and not a mate for marriage. She grieves over him until she meets her enemy that takes her virginity and leaves her with child.

As you know when you become angry it can cause the enemy to come in and destroy your soul. God said watch and pray. She is shamed because she wanted her baby to have a father. When you grieve it can cause you to quit life. She has now turn back to her faith and has made some drastic changes in her life and is willing to wait on the Lord for her mate. It only takes some of us to make one error to find our way and others it takes longer. We thank God for the Woman at the Well because Jesus did not expose her shame but allowed her to drink from the fountain of living water. Wait on the Lord and He will renew your strength (Isaiah 40:31).

Living Water: For he that soweth to his flesh shall of the flesh reap corruption; but he that soweth to the Spirit shall of the spirit reap life everlasting (Galatians 6:8). Be not deceived; God is not mocked: for whatsoever a man soweth, that shall he also reap (Galatians 6:7).

The Weary Soul

There is no rest for the wicked. Life has beaten some of us down because of the pride of life and afflictions. Job replies to his friends after his sickness, "My soul is weary of my life; I will leave my complaints upon myself; I will speak in the bitterness of my soul" (Job 10:1). Hannah cried out in the bitterness of her soul and prayed and God answered her prayer because of the vow she made (1st. Samuel 1:15). In Galatians the Bible tells us not to be weary in well doing: for in due season we shall reap, if we faint not." (Galatians 6:9).

We get tired of our jobs, our marriages, friendships, and trying to please God without the fruit of the spirit. You can become weary with your children because they are not measuring up to society. There many ecosystems out there that can empower us or makes us weary. The only way to fight the weary soul is to put on the Armour of God to fight against the wile of the devil (Ephesians 6:11). We are to be rooted and grounded in the Word.

When you ignore the things of God and go about doing your own thing, the northern army is among you, which is God's Army. The flesh man is there until you bring forth fruit. God said in his word "be fruitful and multiply and replenish the earth and subdue it."(Genesis 1:28). "But I will remove far from you the northern army, and drive him into a land barren and desolate, with his face toward the east sea, and his hinder part toward the utmost sea, and his stink shall come up, and his ill savor shall come up, because he hath done great things." And I will restore to you the years that the locust hath eaten, the cankerworm, and the caterpillar, and the palmerworm, my great army which I sent among you (Joel 2:20,25).

Living Water: There is a water relief for the weary soul. "But they that wait upon the Lord shall renew their strength; they shall mount up with wings as eagles; they shall walk, and not faint" (Isaiah 40:31). He gives power to the faint; and to them that have no might he increaseth strength (Isaiah 40:29).

Odious Woman
(Hateful and Offensive) Proverbs 30:23

The odious woman is one that has been produced by society through hardship and malfunction. Each of us at one point in our lives has been hateful and offensive to others.

In marriage we find her being odious because of her husband's unfaithfulness. She develops low self-esteem through the things she suffers in life. When your husband cheats on you it brings out the bitterness and hatred. His life becomes a living nightmare because of the distrust and unforgiviness. She only cooks when she desires to and refuses to lie with him for fear of disease. When you been dishonored you become offensive to all those that surround you. You start to drink alcohol and look for an affair to get even with your mate.

The children suffer because of your stink. When you are angry it is an ugly scene and it carries an odor. Society does not help because it looks at you as being just like your mother or father. Whatever background they had you feel labeled by their mistakes. There is a generational curse that came upon all those who disobeyed God (Deuteronomy 28:15-68).

As we look at her she has been around for generations. She is a housewife, teacher, nurse, lawyer these are some of her traits but we have been her in our weakness and low points in life. The woman that was bowed down for eighteen years had problems but did not know how to free herself. When Jesus saw her He spoke to her spirit and recognized her as a daughter of Abraham that Satan had bound all those years. He loosed her from her infirmity. The woman with the issues of blood suffered with an odor because of her issue. Sometimes sickness and disease can cause us to become desperate. When you are fearful you do desperate things. She crawled on the ground to reach Jesus' garment and as a result she was made whole (Luke 8:47-48).

Society has labeled her in commercials and exploited her body and femininity as that of being unwholesome. She works in positions that violates her person and causes her to misappropriate her character to please society. Her gracefulness turns into bitterness because she is misunderstood. She is an odious woman that needs a well.

Only Jesus can meet us at the well to tell us truth.

After The Woman at the Well heard truth she left her water pots to tell the story. "She said come see a man that told me all that I ever did: could this be the Christ?"(John 4:29). Jesus came to set the captive free. All those who come to the well will never thirst again. "Jesus said whosoever drinketh of the water that I shall give him shall never thirst; but the water that I shall give him shall be in him a well of water springing up into everlasting life" (John 4:14).

Living Water: There is a water relief for everything that life has to offer. Jesus came to bind up the broken hearted, to proclaim liberty to the captives and opening of the prison to them that are bounds; to proclaim the acceptable year of the Lord, and the day of vengeance of our God; to comfort all that mourn; To appoint unto them that mourn in Zion, to give unto them beauty for ashes, the oil of joy for mourning, the garment of praise for the spirit of heaviness; that they might be called trees of righteousness, The planting of the Lord, that he might be glorified" (Isaiah 61:1-3).

The Twin Identity

The controlling woman has split personalities and is multifaceted. Her lifestyle is rigid, and strict to the order of religion, because of her abuse in early childhood. When you have been manipulated at an early age you become watchful. Everyone that comes into your life looks like the same picture as before. We all have our times in life where we are in control. We are taught to manage our lives and to be disciplined but, sometimes we carry it to the extreme. Each of us has a twin and they both live within us. One obeys the flesh and the other obeys the Spirit of God. The Bible tells us that they that sow to the flesh will reap from the flesh and those that sow to the spirit will reap life everlasting (Galatians 6:8). The spirit man and the flesh man are identical but their lifestyles are different.

The flesh is stiff and unyielding. "The Bible tells us that they that are after the flesh do mind the things of the flesh; but they that after the Spirit the of the Spirit. For to be carnally minded is death; but to be spiritually minded is life and peace. Because the carnal mind is enmity against God: for it is not subject to the law of God, neither indeed can be. So then they that are in the flesh cannot please God" (Romans 8:5-8).

This woman who has lived her life in two places has become an island. Her isolation is her grief. Her husband has divorced her and pride has taken control of her life. She eats excessively has become over weight. She is an animal in a cage that has closed her life to soak in grief. She hides in books. She eats green trees, which is knowledge in excess and bitterness has caused disease in her body. She has need of a well. She is ruling and managing her lifestyle using all the programs of the flesh.

Her Spirit wants to serve the Lord and do those things that are pleasing in his sight, but the flesh man has more control of her life. Her wisdom is self-imposed. Her abuse has caused her to abuse others. She now takes instead of gives and now her friends are few. The Bible states; "But if ye have bitter envying and strife in your hearts, glory not, and lie not against the truth. This wisdom descendeth not from above, but is earthly, sensual, and devilish. For where envying and strife is, there is confusion and every evil work" (James 3:14-16).

But the wisdom that is from above is first pure, then peaceable, gentle, and easy to be entreated, full of mercy and good fruits, without partiality, and without *hypocrisy. And* the fruit of righteousness is sown in peace of them that make peace (James 3:17-18).

The twin is there that you may choose. God has set before us life and death, blessing and cursing: therefore choose life, that both thou and thy seed may live" (Deuteronomy 30:19). The Woman at the Well released her lifestyle to Jesus by leaving her water pot and receiving his words. "He said that the words he speaks are spirit and life (John 6:63).

Living Water: Ye have not chosen me, but I have chosen you, and ordained you, that ye should go and bring forth fruit, and that your fruit should remain: that whatsoever ye ask of the Father in my name, he may give it to you (John 15:16).

The Heartache Woman

This woman has a broken heart and a contrite spirit and a mind to destroy herself and those who hurt her. As you know, in every hate and love relationship there is a soul tie that has not been cut away. Each relationship has its purpose. When we fall in love with the idea of love instead of the love of God we are trapped with our own ideology. Our first love is God but we are not aware of it because it has not been taught.

This woman walks out of her marriage after 20 years and begins to see her childhood sweet heart as her fantasy. She sees her action as being justified by her suffering with an alcoholic. When you have suffered for so many years in this type of relationship you can become bitter. So when your childhood sweetheart comes along and starts talking and energizing your spirit you think it is love. Not realizing the importance of unity you wander away from your problems into the hands of your first love. After a period of time you begin to feel the right thing to do is to leave your husband for another man. After all your feelings have captivated your soul. You release your feelings to your husband and he okays your action and you walk from one world into another. After being married to the childhood sweet heart for three years she discovered that he might be cheating. This brings rage to your soul. Not realizing the same scene that had been done to her first husband reversed itself. What goes around comes again. Her first husband dies and she begins to grieve his death not knowing that she had never released him when she married the second husband. In actuality, she was still married to the first husband.

She would visit his gravesite because of the guilt in her soul. But one day a woman with a well brought her to a woman that drew out of her soul the hidden agenda. She confessed her faults and released her first husband even though he had passed on.

She asked for forgiveness and released him back to God and then she forgave her second husband for his infidelity. She asked God for forgiveness and renewed her vows and received the baptism of the Holy Ghost with the evidence of speaking in tongues. She now has the peace of God that surpasses all her understanding. There will always be a need to drink from the fountain of living waters.

Living Water: But if we walk in the light as He is in the light, we have fellowship one with another, and the blood of Jesus Christ his Son cleanseth us from all sin. If we say that we have no sin, we deceive ourselves, and the truth is not in us. If we confess our sins, He is faithful and just to forgive us our sins, and cleanse us from all unrighteousness (1 John 1:7-9).

Overcoming Women

"These things I have spoken unto you, that in me ye might have peace. In the world ye shall have tribulation: but be of good cheer; I have overcome the world."
(John 16:33)

Woman at the Well

Overcoming Women

The overcoming woman has her mind made up and her actions speak louder than her words. She positions herself for destiny. She has found her true love. She refuses to look back but presses on into the higher calling. She is one that stands in the battle and knows that God is who He is. She prays and spends quality time with God.

Overcoming is when you lose your closest friend - your mother and before you can feel the void He places a newborn in the womb. After that the doctor tells you that your baby will be born with Down syndrome and later tells you that the baby has a tumor on the brain. She looks the devil in the face of the trial and says, "let every man be a liar and God's word be true" (Romans 3:4). She is a wonder because her love for God is greater than any circumstances. Her mind is adamant and her unwavering faith has given her favor. When you begin to believe God you get the results of believing.

She knows that he is her Shield, her Buckler and Hightower (Psalm 18:2). She knows that no weapon formed against her shall prosper and what ever she does shall prosper (Isaiah 54:17).

She knows that she is a light that sits on a hill that cannot be hid (Matthew 5:14). He is the bright and morning star (Revelation 22:16) and her thoughts are true, honest, just, pure, lovely and of a good report (Philippians 4:8). She knows that her life is in the hand of the potter and that he makes us over and over again (Jeremiah 18:6). She knows that God takes pleasure in blessing his children (Psalm 35:27).

She has overcome by the word of her testimony (Revelation 12:11).

Living Water: For whosoever is born of God overcometh the world: and this is the victory that overcometh the world, even our faith (1John 5:4). He that overcometh shall inherit all things; and I will be his God, and he shall be my son (Revelation 21:7).

> *"If ye love me,
> keep my commandments."*
> *(John 14:15)*

Woman of Submission

A woman of submission is one of great price. She is clothed in tapestry of many colors. Her beauty is exhibited through her obedience. She is meek and full of compassion. Her house is built on love. Who can find a virtuous woman? For her price is far above rubies (Proverbs 31:10).

Every wise woman buildeth her house: but the foolish plucketh it down with her hands (Proverbs 14:1) "Likewise, you wives, be in subjection to your own husbands; that, if any obey not the word, they also may be won by the conversation of the wives; while they behold your chaste conversation couple with fear. Whose adoring let it not be that outward adoring of plaiting the hair, and of wearing of gold, or of putting on of apparel; but let it be the hidden man of the heart, in that which is not corruptible, even the ornament of a meek and quiet spirit, which is in the sight of God of great price"
(1Peter 3:1-4).

"Likewise, you husbands, dwell with them according to knowledge, giving honor unto the wife, as unto the weaker vessel, and as being heirs together of the grace of life; that your prayers be not hindered" (1Peter 3:7).

A woman of submission is wise. When wisdom entereth into thine heart, and knowledge is pleasant unto thy soul; discretion shall preserve thee, understanding shall keep thee: to deliver thee from the evil man, from the man that speak the forward things (Proverbs 2:10-11).

As we look at her we can see her character is godly and she is a woman that the Lord favors. "She is a tree of life to them that lay hold upon her: and happy is every one that retaineth her. Her ways are ways of pleasantness, and all her paths are peace. Length of days is in her right hand; and in her left hand riches and honour" (Proverbs 3:18,

17, 16). The woman of submission is a churchwoman of wisdom that has submitted her life to Christ.

Living Water: Therefore, as the church is subject unto Christ, so let the wives be to their own husbands in every thing. Husbands love your wives, even as Christ so loved the church, and gave himself for it; that he might sanctify and cleanse it with the washing of water by the word, that he might present it to himself a glorious church, not having spot, or wrinkle, or any such thing; but that it should be holy and without blemish (Ephesians 5:24-27).

Deborah

Deborah a mighty woman of God dedicated to the purpose of God waits on the moving of the Holy Spirit. She serves her community as she sits under a palm tree. She steps up to the plate to fight for the cause. Much has been given to her. She is a Prophetess, a Judge, a messenger, a warrior, a mother and a well of life. Her position is respected because God chose her. Where much is given much is required (Luke 12:48).

She was not trying to be this or that but labored with simplicity. When you know who you are in God you can respond to your calling with great dedication. Deborah's mannerism was of tenderness and great mercy. She had compassion. Her office for counseling was under the tree of life. God said he was the true vine and we are the branches (John 15:1). All those who came to her found answers to their problems.

As the virtuous woman Deborah was married but her calling did not interfere with duties to her husband. The Bible tells us to submit ourselves to one another in the fear of the Lord (Ephesians 5:21). With all the hats she wore her dedication was with great boldness.

The children of Israel cried out to God because the hand of the king Jabin of Canaan was upon them. They had done evil in the site of the Lord. Deborah sent for Barak and said unto him, "hath not the Lord God of Israel commanded, saying go and draw toward mount Tabor, and take with thee ten thousand men of the children of Napthtali and of the children of Zebulun?" And I will draw unto thee to the river Kison Sisera, the captain of Jabin's army, with his chariots and his multitude; and I will deliver him into thine hand" (Judges 4:6-7). Deborah had such devotion and commitment that "Barak said to her, if thou wilt go with me, then I will go: but if thou wilt not go with me, then I will not go" (Judges 4:8). Deborah made it clear to Barak that he would not be honored, but that the Lord would put Sisera into the hand of a woman."

Jael was also a dedicated woman of purpose who was "blessed above women" and she destroyed Sisera with a hammer she smote of his head and pierced through his temple (Judges 5:26). She was called blessed for her deeds. When a man does not walk in his calling a "woman shall compass a man" (Jeremiah 31:22).

When we don't walk in the promises of God we fall prey to the enemy of this world. The children of Israel had not conquered all the land in Canaan. Instead they walk in their ways and fell into sin. But through the dedication of Deborah and Barak, and Jael Israel rested for forty years. When you are resting you are able to sing the songs of victory. They praised God for avenging their enemies. When you love God you will obey and walk in dedication.

Living Water: I am the vine, you are the branches: He that abides in me, and I in him, the same bring forth much fruit: for without me you can do nothing (John 15:5). Jesus said "If a man love me, he will keep my words: and my Father will love him, and we will come unto him, and make our abode with him" (John 14:23).

Grandmothers Challenges

Grandmothers in this season of life who are raising grandchildren are challenged by life's expectations. When your children have become negligent with drugs and alcohol or develop a disease called AIDS and are no longer capable of caring for her children, this is a touching situation for the grandmothers who did not expect to start a new life raising grandchildren. She is forced to take the children or they will be turned over to foster homes to have strangers raise them. This can be a bitter and resentful life. We love our grandchildren but in some cases they don't have the proper assets and home status, some are under the poverty level because some grandparents are ill and need health care yet they are the only caregivers.

When the test of trial comes in life whether you are a believer or not the word will be tried. "The word of the Lord is tried, and he is a buckler to all those who trust in him" (Psalm 18:31). Everything goes back to The Woman at the Well who had need of the fountain of living water. Without this water we cannot be released from the traumas of life. This is a job for Jesus because without him you can do nothing (John 15:5).

Grandmothers of yesteryear were warriors that fought the battles with courage and stability. These were women that put their children in front and walked behind them to make sure they were protected. There are times when we are not watchful that the enemy comes in to destroy our children. The Bible tells us to watch and pray (Mark 14:38). These grandmothers prayed to God day and night. They were homemakers who taught their children homemaking skills and how to be parents. And all thy children *shall be* taught of the Lord; and great *shall be* the peace of thy children (Isaiah 54:13).

The influence of the grandmothers gave them light. As we know each generation has it purpose but this season of women were strong in the Lord. Let us not forget the strength that God has poured into us through his Son Jesus. Remember the days of old; consider the years of many generations (Deuteronomy 32:7). And these words, which I command thee this day, shall be in thine heart: And thou shalt teach them diligently unto thy children, and shalt talk of them when thou sittest in thine house, and when thou walkest by the way, and when thou liest down and when thou risest up. And thou shalt bind them for a sign upon thine hand, and they shall be as frontlets between thine eyes (Deuteronomy 6:6-8). God commanded us to teach our children so they would know His statues. They were to love the Lord thy God with all thine heart, and with all thy soul, and with all thy might (Deuteronomy 6:5).

Living Water: Train up a child in the way he should go: and when he is old, he will not depart from it (Proverbs 22:1).

Anna (Prophetess)

Anna was a dedicated woman that was well favored. She prayed day and night. As we look at her the bible does not talk about her at length but her lifestyle speaks for her. We know that she love God because she was devoted in her action. As we have learned in our life experiences that action speaks louder than words. The Bible tells us that whatsoever ye do in word or deed; do all in the name of the Lord Jesus, giving thanks to God and the Father by him (Colossians 3:17).

She was a prophetess, the daughter of Phanuel, of the tribe of Aser: she was of great age, and had lived with an husband seven years from her virginity; And she was a widow of about fourscore and four years (84), which departed not from the temple, but served God with fasting and prayers night and day (Luke 2:36-37). Her focus was on the redemption in Jerusalem.

As we look at this powerful woman we see that she gave up her life to serve the Lord. She had the spirit of prayer and she stood in the gap for her people.

Her age says something about dedication. When we know our purpose in life we can enjoy the things of God. Anna knew her purpose and her calling. She walked in the kindness and showed mercy to the people of Israel. The Bible tells us as she prayed and "gave thanks to the Lord, and spoke of him to all them that looked for redemption in Jerusalem" (Luke 2:38). We thank God for this woman who was committed to the purpose of serving. Jesus said for whether is greater, he that sitteth at meat, or he that serveth? But I am among you that serveth (Luke 22:27). Anna understood the character of Christ and she drank from the fountain of living water day and night.

Living Water: No servant can serve two masters: for either he will hate the one, and love the other; or else he will hold to the one, and despise the other. You cannot serve God and mammon (Luke 16:13). If any man serve me, let him follow me; and where I am, there shall also my servant be: if any man serve me, him will my Father honour (John 12:26).

Naomi

Naomi was a dedicated woman who had many losses that left her with the taste of bitterness. Let us look at her from the other side of her bitterness. We know that she was hurt because of her many losses but, there is another side of her that's devoted to the purpose that God intended her to be. Out of all our frustrations and disappointments in life comes the anointing. When the olives are crushed they bring forth oil that heals. She is a woman of strength and beauty and her tenderness and kindness drew her daughter in-law to follow her into a strange land. According to the Hebrew Dictionary (5278) her name means delight, suitableness, splendor, grace, beauty and pleasantness. Through her losses she returns to her home in Bethlehem, which is the house of bread according to Hebrew (1035). She had such a beauty about her that her daughter in-law reverences her as a mother.

Naomi instructs Ruth:

She instructs her daughter in-law to glean only in the field of Boaz because he was a near kinsman. The Bible speaks of the older woman teaching the younger woman how to love her husband. She was seasoned and understood the principles of her forefathers. She gave Ruth insight how to go on the threshing floor at the feet of Boaz. Boaz is a type of Christ that we come humbly before the throne of grace. She said unto her "wash thyself therefore, and anoint thee, and put thy raiment upon thee, and get down to the floor: but make thyself known unto the man, until he shall have done eating and drinking". 'And it shall be, when he lie down, that thou shall mark the place where he shall lie, and thou shall go in, and uncover his feet, and lay thee down; and he will tell thee what thou shall do" (Ruth 3:3-4).

As we lay before the Lord He will let us know that whatever the enemy meant for evil that He would turn it around. And we know that all things work together for good to them that love God, to them who are the called according to His purpose (Romans 8:28). She laid at the feet of Boaz until morning and returned to her mother-in-law with six measures of barley. "He that comes to God must believe that he is, and that he is a rewarder of them that diligently seek Him" (Hebrew 11:6) Ruth obeyed her mother-in-law and was honored by Boaz.

Naomi is a well that was prepared before the foundation of the world to teach Ruth how to walk in the divine life of her destiny. She gained wisdom, knowledge, and mercy. God honored her lineage because it brought forth kings out of her lions.

Living Water: Let us come boldly unto the throne of grace that we may obtain mercy, and find grace to help in time of need (Hebrew 4:16).

The Program Woman

This woman has a whole line of programs because of the teaching she has received. She is multifaceted and has become bitter and resentful because she can't get a hold of her inheritance. Religion has gotten the best of her during her visits to many organizations to find truth. Her attempt has not been successful. There are several layers of walls that built a fortress in her soul.

The bitterness creeps into her marriage and also her relationships. She is always looking for a word to minimize the last word. The world at large is her standard of living. She has been misunderstood by many and her grip on life has not held her stable. As we look at her we know that her character has been displayed in many areas of life. The Bible tells us that he that come to God must believe that He is, and that he is a rewarder of them that diligently seek Him (Hebrew 11:6). She walks in false identity and is separated from herself. She collects knowledge but never learning, and never able to come to the knowledge of the truth (2 Timothy 3:6). She hides in goals that she creates for herself.

Her self-esteem is governed by her systematic way of doing things. She is possessive and brings the madness into her marriage. She will not stay married because of the demand she places upon her mate. When you are never satisfied in life you elude to programs to satisfy your needs. Some join different clubs and other organizations to keep the mind occupied. This woman feels that no one can understand her but God who is rich in mercy and died that we may walk in divine light (Ephesians 2:4). This is a job for Jesus. Jesus came to deliver us from all the ordinances of man.

As you know culture is born from one generation to the next. Whatever they handed down falls upon that generation. There are underlining issues, Comparison ancestry doubt and unbelief that was spoken over their life. God sent His son Jesus to "break down the middle wall petition between us; having abolish in His flesh the enmity, even the law of commandments contained in ordinances; to make in himself of twain one new man, so making peace" (Ephesians 2:14-15).

The Woman at the Well was also programmed and thought that no one understood her problem or condition. As you know when you are hurting you begin to think that your situation is unsolvable but God can do all things. "He can do exceeding abundantly above all that we ask or think, according to the power that works in us: (Ephesians 3:20). As we look at the Woman at the Well we can see the mercy of the Lord. He did not expose her shame but poured into her mercy and truth.

His mercy endures forever (Psalm 107:1).

Living Water: Seek first the kingdom of God and His righteousness; and all these things shall be added unto you" (Matthew 6:33).

The Bleeding Woman of Grief

This woman has carried grief in her soul for so many years. She walks in life as if it were her clothing. Bitterness sets in due to her taking care of a sick loved one. This attitude in her life has caused her to become even bitter with God. Her bleeding is so intense that she takes it into her work place. She strives at being excellent to hide her emotions. As you know when you are hurting you become controlling and when the love one is your husband it is a greater offense. When offence comes it separates you from society because you are forever in fear of what's going to happen or when it will happen. The Bible tells us "as man think in his heart so is he" (Proverbs 23:7). Grief sets in through our thought process. Without the mind of Christ we will fall for anything.

Through her grief she becomes suicidal and her behavior is not appropriate. Her disposition changes after years of torment. Depression sets in and causes her to have low-self esteem and what was once an excellent spirit becomes complacent. This attitude will cause us to bleed. When you are bleeding you have unanswered issues. It takes a well of water to clean and purge out the old leaven. Our past can become our future if we don't let it go. Paul said "brethren, I count not myself to have apprehended: but this one thing I do, forgetting those things which are behind, and reaching forth unto those things which are before, I press toward the mark for the prize of the high calling of God in Christ Jesus" (Philippians 3:13-14).

Only God can stop the bleeding. When we cry out God hears. He said call upon me in a time of trouble and I will be "a present help" (Psalms 46:1). This bleeding woman meets a well; a woman that speaks into her life and tells her of the hidden grief. Her husband had died and left her and she resented it. She had no closure because she was still holding on to some of his stuff. As you know as long as we hold on to the past the future cannot unfold. When you are waiting on a mate and its not happening just check out what's in your soul. Our will, mind, and emotions are there to keep us frail if we don't allow Christ to be Lord. God delivered the bleeding woman after she had cried out to him and as he heard Hannah He also heard her. She recognized what had happened and God opened up her spiritual eyes that she could see clearly. She has recovered and is on her way to the position God has called her to. What a God we serve!

Living Water: God is in the midst of her: she shall not be moved: God shall help her, and that right early" (Psalms 46:5). "Trust in the Lord with all thine heart; and lean not unto thine own understanding." In all thy ways acknowledge Him, and he shall direct thy paths (Proverbs 3:5-6).

Insecure Woman

The insecure woman is a needy woman that always needs some one to confirm her. She is fearful of failing and continually need a word. She hides in religion and she manipulates her friends. She is deceitful and dishonest. We have all been her at one point in our lives because we have been lacking in confidence and needed someone to affirm us. As we look at her we can see if we have put her to death. She is a leaky woman and whatever you say to her in comfort she still looks for more answers. She is never satisfied. She takes this madness into relationships and her self-esteem is lowered because she does not trust anyone. She holds on to past experiences and her heart is a heart of unforgiviness. She is selfish and thinks that her motives in life are the right motives to live by. She is walking on eggshells because she knows what she used to do. God is not speaking and so she feels the oasis of being in the desert.

She lacks confidence in God because He is stripping her and rebuilding her personality. Her insecurity in her new spirit is not intentional but she is looking for direction. The insecure woman is the flesh woman that has not put her confidence in God. She has been saved but has not made Jesus her Lord. As you know this is a walk by faith and not by sight (2 Corinthians 5:7). God said without Faith it is impossible to please him (Hebrew 11:6).

Living Water: Cast not away therefore your confidence, which hath great recompense of reward. For ye have need of patience, that, after ye have done the will of God, ye might receive the promise (Hebrew 10:35-36).

> "Jesus saith unto him, I am the way, the truth, and the life: no man cometh unto the Father, but by me."
> (John 14:6)

The Stage Woman

This woman is one that has been through many transitions. She has developed a tree. As you know each step we take in life is a necessity to arrive at the next plateau. Baby steps are our first stage in our process of development because each step is growth and each step has purpose. As you go up the ladder remember to put your feet on each step. This is growing time and each step is a development in God. This woman has tried to avoid her steps but we all must go through the stages of life. The stage of trust verses mistrust is based on our relationships with our parents or our husbands and also friends who have betrayed us. When you are taking your first step in marriage you are trusting in your mate just, as you trusted in your mother and father as you took the first step to walk. If we missed this stage it can cause us to make unwise decisions in life to come.

This stage woman has missed some growing steps and her childhood has crippled her in her soul. She has lost the trust of her mother and father. She walked from childhood into adulthood. She brings this undeveloped spirit into her marriage and through years of despair she hangs up the harps. She commits suicide in her mind and every child conceived is aborted. There are no bowels for mercy because of shame.

This is shame that we experience in life that throws a curve at us as we journey. It's when we lose control that we are disgraced and become doubtful. We lose control and live in guilt because of the abuse we have experienced. We begin to think that everything that happens to us is our fault. We develop an inferiority complex when we no longer can function in our capacity. During this stage we grow in multiple personalities. When you don't know who you are you can fall for anything. This stage helps you build character in stability and assurance. When you are identifying yourself in society there are roles we portray in religion, workforce, relationships and economics and when we refuse our identity we bring in confusion.

Intimacy and isolation is a stage that we have experienced also love and rejection. The love is the feelings of acceptance but isolation is being rejected from a mate, close friend or family. This stage deals with our emotions and frustrations. During this time we look for doors to find a resting place but until we faced the steps there is no rest. As we know the Bible tells us that Jesus said, "I will never leave you nor forsake you" (Hebrew 13:5).

Integrity is one of the greatest steps to take and this stage is the one step that has been manipulated by the ones we trust the most. This step is one that will bring us to a higher level in God. "The just man walk in his integrity: his children are blessed after him" (Proverbs 20:7). God sees our heart and He knows the ones that trust in Him.

Resilience is the spirit that has kept this woman who experienced the hardness in life. This is a built in mechanism that takes us to a higher step without missing the bottom ladder. She is rejected and isolated because she refuses to give up. Her stages are stages of triumph. We are more than conquerors through him that loved us (Romans 8:38).

Anticipated and unanticipated transitions are transitions that we expect and don't expect. One of our steps in anticipated is a good marriage, a perfect ministry, and children of high caliber. Our unanticipated is when the husband becomes ill after you have been married for three months. He had to have surgery and loss wages from his job and finally had to retire. This is an alarming situation, which you did not anticipate, but was able to get through the transition with prayer and support from friends. Our children that begin to take drugs fall into trouble with the law is not what we expected and also our ministry that falls into slander from a close brother or sister in the church. These are transitions that bring you closer to God and closer to your spouses and friends and family.

Although we didn't label Jezebel in any of these stages she is hidden in each of these women waiting at the well.

These are stages and cycles in life that we can go back and reflect on because it was apart of our learning experience. My husband always says, "It's a learning way." The value of development is to be taught of the Lord.

Living Water: And all thy children shall be taught of the Lord; and great shall be the peace of thy children. In righteousness shalt thou be established: thou shalt be far from oppression; for thou shalt not fear: and from terror; for it shall not come near thee" (Isaiah 54:13-14).

> "Beloved, if God so loved us, we ought also to love one another."
> (1 John 4:11)

Red Hat Women

The Red hat women have been seasoned. They are over fifty and have seen life in many facets. They are now reigning in their jubilee. They are now celebrating life instead of struggling with life. As we know from the biblical prospective the color purple is for royalty and the color red is life. Each group of women are from all walks of life but the one thing they all have in common is that they are all over fifty. Being of the same age or older these women are talented and gifted and helpers of one another.

Their next journey will be one of excitement because they have been spirited in strength, courage, and stability. They are energetic and very powerful women who have been nourished in life with wisdom and understanding.

When you have organized your life with character structure your children will call you blessed. You are like the tree that's been planted by the waters that will bring forth fruit in their season; their leaf also shall not wither and whatsoever they do shall prosper (Psalms 1:3).

These women are in the prime of their life and having fun has become a priority. As we grow in life we find that we have left some of our stages behind. Anytime you grow there will be steps to take and every one is different in their growth and development. If we miss a step we will have go back find the missing step. As a red hatter I find that life at work and life in the home has left some of us bankrupt. We are experiencing steps that were missing over the years. We are now able to do things that bring joy to our lives. Just going to dinner with a friend, having tea with a group of women from all walks of life, or going to a museum or, taking boat ride down the river while sharing a dream with a friend, or writing books and sending cards to a secret pal has completed some of these steps.

When these women go out in society they are dressed so beautifully that those who are passing by take notice. Like any new fad there will be some talk but what I really like about them they all have so much in common they are searching for the same gift and that's love. Some are widows and some need to talk and some need a friend. We all want to be celebrated in life and as the red hatter used the talents and gifts that God has given to them they are sharing their life. Some of the woman have not valued their life and have not known how wonderful they are made in the eyes of God. I wanted them to know that God loves them and they are being celebrated for this season of time and that taking time to smell the roses is a gift from God. Hats off to the Red Hat Women!

Living Water: And you shall hallow the fiftieth year, and proclaim liberty throughout all the land unto all the inhabitants thereof: it shall be a jubilee unto you; and you shall return every man unto his possession, and you shall return every man unto his family. A jubilee shall that fiftieth year be unto you: you shall not sow; neither reap that which groweth of itself in it, nor gather the grapes in it of thy vine undresses. For it is the jubilee; it shall be holy unto you: you shall eat the increase thereof out of the field (Leviticus 25:10-12).

The Virtuous Woman (Proverbs 31)

This woman has the capacity to do many tasks without complaining. The Bible opens her up as saying, "Who can find a virtuous woman?" For her price is far above rubies.

The heart of her husband doth safely trust in her, so that he shall have no need of spoil. She will do him good and not evil all the days of her life.

She seeks wool, and flax, and work willingly with her hands. She is like the merchants' ships; she brings her food from afar.

She rises also while it is yet night, and gives meat to her household, and portion to her maidens.

She considereth a field, and buys it: with the fruit of her hands she planted a vineyard. She girded her lions with strength, and strengthened her arms. She perceived that her merchandise is good: her candle goeth not out by night.

She lay her hands to the spindle, and her hands hold the distaff. She stretches out her hand to the poor; yea, she reaches forth her hands to the needy.

She is not afraid of the snow for her household: for all her household are clothed with scarlet. She makes herself coverings of tapestry; her clothing is silk and purple.

Her husband is known in the gates, when he sits among the elders of the land. She makes fine linen, and sells it; and delivers girdles unto the merchant.

Strength and honor are her clothing; and she shall rejoice in time to come. She opens her mouth with wisdom; and in her tongue is the law of kindness. She looks well to the ways of her household, and eat not the bread of idleness. Her children arise up and, and call her blessed; her husband also praise her.

Many daughters have done virtuously, but thou excellest them all. Favour is deceitful, and beauty is vain: but a woman that fears the Lord, she shall be praised.

Give her of the fruit of her hands; and let her own works praise her in the gates.

Living Water: I will praise thee; for I am fearfully and wonderfully made: marvelous are thy works; and that my soul knoweth right well (Psalm 139:14). Who so findeth a wife findeth a good thing, and obtained favour of the Lord (Proverbs 18:22).

This book was birthed out of the fruit of my labor and the journey is one of a lifetime commitment to the King of kings and the Lord of lords.

About the Author

Pastor Evelyn Sanders is the author of three books and co-author of one. She is a student, a teacher, and president and founder of Come and See Ministries Inc. Her new endeavor includes seminars and consulting. She has a degree in Human Services from Springfield College in Springfield, Massachusetts. Pastor Sanders is presently enrolled at International Masters Divinity School in Evansville Indiana to obtain her Master of Ministry in Christian Studies with a focus on Biblical counseling. Her goal is to bring many souls into the kingdom. She shares with her husband, Pastor Richard Sanders, ministering and teaching in Come and See Ministries, Inc. They are both dedicated to the purpose which God has called them. The Sanders have two sons, one daughter (deceased) and five lovely grandchildren.

For more information or copies of this book:

Please contact:
Pastor Evelyn Sanders
11 Calvin Street
Springfield MA 01104
(413) 733-9578

or

Come and See Ministries
120 Carando Drive
Springfield MA 01104
(413) 205-1453

rievsanders@msn.com
20.00/book +5.00 S&H (soft cover)
25.99/book +5.00 S&H (hard cover)

PASTOR EVELYN SANDERS
11 CALVIN ST
SPRINGFIELD, MA 01104
EVELYN_SANDERS_11@MSN.COM

> "Blessed are they which do hunger
> and thirst after righteousness:
> for they shall be filled."
> (Matthew 5:6)

"And all my children shall be taught of the Lord; and great shall be the peace of thy children."
(Isaiah 54:13).